MARKETING
YOUR
STARTUP

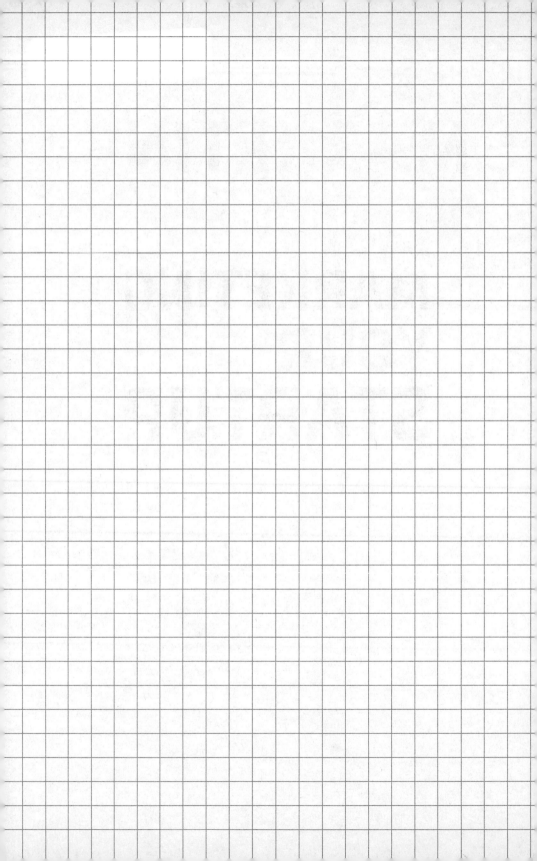

MARKETING YOUR STARTUP

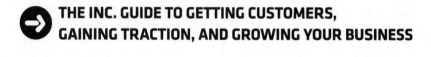

**THE INC. GUIDE TO GETTING CUSTOMERS,
GAINING TRACTION, AND GROWING YOUR BUSINESS**

Simona Covel

AMACOM

AMERICAN MANAGEMENT ASSOCIATION

New York • Atlanta • Brussels • Chicago • Mexico City • San Francisco
Shanghai • Tokyo • Toronto • Washington, D. C.

This publication is designed to provide accurate and authoritative information in regard to the subject matter covered. It is sold with the understanding that the publisher is not engaged in rendering legal, accounting, or other professional service. If legal advice or other expert assistance is required, the services of a competent professional person should be sought.

Library of Congress Cataloging-in-Publication Data

Names: Covel, Simona, author.
Title: Marketing your startup : the inc. guide to getting customers, gaining
   traction, and growing your business / Simona Covel.
Description: New York : AMACOM, [2018] | Includes index.
Identifiers: LCCN 2017060023 (print) | LCCN 2018004101 (ebook) | ISBN
   9780814439685 (ebook) | ISBN 9780814439302 (pbk.)
Subjects: LCSH: New business enterprises--Marketing.
Classification: LCC HD62.5 (ebook) | LCC HD62.5 .C675 2018 (print) | DDC
   658.8--dc23

LC record available at https://lccn.loc.gov/2017060023

About AMA
American Management Association (www.amanet.org) is a world leader in talent development, advancing the skills of individuals to drive business success. Our mission is to support the goals of individuals and organizations through a complete range of products and services, including classroom and virtual seminars, webcasts, webinars, podcasts, conferences, corporate and government solutions, business books, and research. AMA's approach to improving performance combines experiential learning—learning through doing—with opportunities for ongoing professional growth at every step of one's career journey.

10 9 8 7 6 5 4 3 2 1

>>>> **CONTENTS**

>>>> **ACKNOWLEDGMENTS**

WHEN WE SET OUT to write a book that could serve as an easy-to-read, hands-on marketing resource for company founders, we found much of the best material was within our own walls.

For nearly forty years, *Inc.* has provided advice, education, and inspiration to the leaders of fast-growing private companies, chiefly through our unrivaled editorial content.

That material—produced by veteran reporters, all-star editors, and expert columnists, among others—is much of what you see on the pages of this book. Our thanks to all of them; this book wouldn't be possible without their groundbreaking work.

From that reporting, we've compiled the following best-of guide—a book that's both actionable and inspiring, designed to help company founders demystify the art and science of great marketing. Our hope is that this will become a one-stop, indispensable resource to help you spread the word and ignite growth at your company.

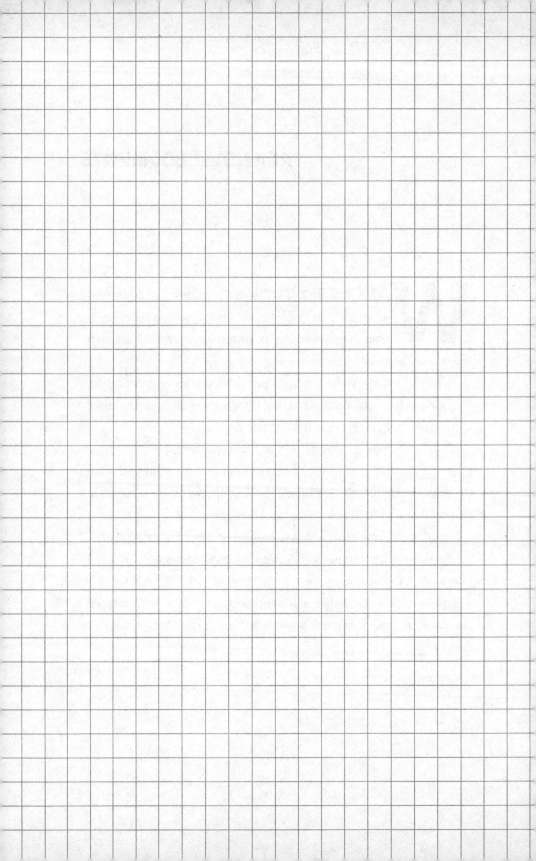

WHAT IF DOLLAR SHAVE Club's founder hadn't made that famous YouTube video, the one where he deadpans about razors, polio, and his big-name competition—to the tune of 25 million views? What if Dropbox didn't think a referral program was worth it—a program that at times, generated 35 percent of the company's signups?[1] What if Warby Parker's PR firm hadn't helped place a story in *GQ*—a piece that dubbed the company the "Netflix of eyewear" and generated so many sales that the startup ran out of inventory?[2]

If those companies' founders hadn't decided to spread the word about their companies—each in their own way—they may have never become household names.

The same goes for your business. So you have a killer product. Now, how will people find out about it?

Many startups fail—even if they offer a great product or groundbreaking service—because they fail to get the word out. They may think the product will sell itself. Or they may think marketing is somehow underhanded, or dirty.

If that describes you, it may help to reframe your idea of marketing. The best marketing isn't about pushing a message or coming up with a slogan. Marketing exists to help you find people who love your product: If you don't plan to invest in marketing, you probably shouldn't invest in building a product, either.

If you're in the early stages of your business, know that it's never too early to start. If you're worried about somebody stealing your product idea, consider another worry, says Dharmesh Shah, co-founder of HubSpot and a small-business marketing expert.[3] Worry about how you'll get customers. And team members. And funding. All of these things are really hard—especially if you don't talk about your idea.

If you're a marketing skeptic, you may have a gut feeling that marketing is sleazy. You're not alone. This book is designed to help you overcome that—to think about marketing in a new way. The best marketing is about building brand, reach, and credibility, and doing what you do best: helping customers.

We know a lot about that: For nearly forty years, *Inc.* has chronicled the victories of fast-growth small businesses—and the bumps along the way. Over the years, we've talked to thousands of founders who grew their companies into household names about how they spread the word.

We learned something essential along the way: You won't win in the marketplace by shouting louder, placing bigger ads, or buying the fanciest booth at a trade show. You'll win by building a marketing strategy and applying the right mix of tactics for your business—no matter your budget.

Let's get started.

WHAT IS MARKETING ANYWAY?

MARKETING IS SURPRISINGLY difficult to define. Part research, part design, part sales—at its core, marketing is any activity that makes it easier to sell your product. We're talking generating leads, running TV ads, using customer relationship management software, or authoring a blog: It all falls under the marketing umbrella.

You've probably heard people use the terms marketing, advertising, and branding interchangeably. But if you want marketing to help drive your sales, you first need to understand the differences.

MARKETING

Let's start with marketing because it is the umbrella under which all of these other practices live. It includes branding, messaging, online presence, content, social media, PR, advertising, research ... you name it, it lives under the broader canopy of marketing.

BRANDING

Branding refers to the visual elements of a company—but it doesn't stop there. Branding refers to specific elements that range from the logo to the color theory and how the logo is used on different marketing collateral, which is just a fancy name for websites, business cards, and letterhead.

But your brand is broader than your logo—it's about how your company makes people feel. The feeling that you evoke is at the heart of your brand. That can translate into the music in your stores, the chairs you choose for your conference rooms, or what your executives wear.

If you're an engineer or a researcher, the idea of devoting a meaningful amount of mental energy to a logo or a music choice may seem slightly bananas. But the brand is one of the most important parts of developing and invigorating your company. It's all about what emotions you want someone to feel when they come into initial contact—which is critically important for a startup, which hasn't made any kind of impression yet.

Some say it's just a logo . . . tell that to Nike.

What I would do with an extra $10,000 for marketing:

" If I was a new lifestyle company, I'd spend it on branding. Having strong creative with a really crisp point of view that is timeless and stands out, and that you feel reflects who you are as a company, provides huge bang for the buck. You're going to live with your logo for a long time."

——

AMANDA HESSER, founder, *Food52*

PR

❝ It takes 20 years to build a reputation and five minutes to ruin it. If you think about that, you'll do things differently."

—

WARREN BUFFETT

PR, or public relations, is all about getting your brand out there into the press—a category that includes newspapers, magazines and TV but also the ever-growing universe of online media. Done right, PR can be incredibly powerful. Just ask Warby Parker co-founder Neil Blumenthal. Within 48 hours of *GQ* dubbing the company "the Netflix of eyewear" in 2010, the site was so flooded with orders for $95 glasses that Blumenthal temporarily suspended the home try-on program.

That wasn't their only problem. The company had launched the website so quickly that they hadn't included a sold-out indicator—so customers were placing orders long after inventory had run out. The bad news: The waitlist was 20,000 people long. The good news: The company hit its first-year sales target in three weeks. That's the power of your name in the press.

While PR can help give you enviable problems like these, it doesn't work for everyone, and it has to be executed adeptly. Not all media "hits" are created equal. PR is only one of the marketing tools, and in order to be effective, you have to have a great online presence and consumer standing to back it up.

ADVERTISING

Like PR, advertising is an outbound marketing approach—you're pushing your message out. But this time, you're not filtering it through a reporter. With the wonderful world of digital, there are boundless new opportunities to use this space that are extremely cost effective—from traditional media advertising, like billboards and TV, to Google AdWords and the latest social media advertising.

Like PR, it's important to pick advertising destinations that engage your target market. Online advertising in particular can be incredibly granular—allowing you to laser-focus on the specific demographics and even the mindset of your target market. It's also critical to understand that when it comes to the Wild West of social media advertising, the landscape is constantly changing. What worked one month may not work the next, and keeping up with the universe of social media advertising products can feel like a full-time job.

PUTTING IT ALL TOGETHER

All of these disciplines can exist in a silo—but they shouldn't. You likely need a sprinkle of this and a sprinkle of that. Much more importantly, you need a cohesive strategy behind it all in order to determine how much money and muscle to put behind each campaign or initiative.

With such a vast set of objectives, one of the most critical tasks in practicing any kind of marketing is setting aside the time to analyze what worked, what didn't, and what you can do next time to improve performance. If you don't take this time after a campaign or even a test, you'll never get better.

Ultimately, while marketing is an umbrella which encompasses all of the above and more, the handle of that umbrella is sales. All of your marketing messaging should work together and have strong calls to action to drive bottom-line revenue.

Which channels and tactics are right for your company? By the time you finish reading this book, you'll know how to put together a strategy that makes sense for you—whether you've allocated a big part of your budget to marketing or need to bootstrap your way to success.

2

DEFINE YOUR BRAND

ICONIC FITNESS BRAND SOULCYCLE operates indoor cycling studios around the country and helped popularize the pay-per-class fitness model. Founders Julie Rice and Elizabeth Cutler always had a very clear vision of what their brand embodies. According to Rice: When it comes to the brand, she—yes, she—was a person, with distinct needs. "There were no accidents," Rice told *Inc.* "We always thought of SoulCycle as a brand, even when we had no right to think of it as a brand."

That meant laboring over everything from the fonts to the logo to the smell in the studio. Because the company's first location in New York City was set back from the street with no signage, the founders were forced to focus relentlessly on the in-studio experience. "There were no sensory details left unturned," Rice says.

The founders focused obsessively on their customer—the centerpiece of their brand. "We always say when we train employees that we're not looking to create users, we're looking for evangelists. It should be the kind of experience that when you're done and you're going out to dinner with your friends at night you're still talking about it and it takes up most of the dinner conversation." They remembered personal details about customers and went as far as moving a customer's car if her meter was up. That, they say, is the "culture of yes" that makes customers want to tell their friends all about the experience.

From the beginning, they decided SoulCycle would be the star of SoulCycle. The company refused to sell water or protein bars from other makers in their store. Rice says that's a cornerstone of how the brand developed into such a strong presence. "There's only one thing you're ever served, and that is soul. Your shoes say SoulCycle, the wall says SoulCycle, the clothing says SoulCycle. You cannot miss the message that we are trying to deliver you."

SoulCycle's branding works because it starts with the core understanding of their target customer—the person they needed more than any other, day in and day out. Every decision the founders made about the brand was based on connecting with that person—someone who was looking not just to work out, but to connect with a truly immersive experience. That brand became the grounding principle for how the company interacted with customers, every single day.

From there, they relentlessly focused on consistency, which experts say is key. The more consistent you are with every element of your brand—in SoulCycle's case, that even includes the smell of the studios—the more your consumers know exactly who you are and will remain loyal to you.

BRINGING YOUR BRAND TO LIFE

" If people believe they share values with a company, they will stay loyal to the brand."

HOWARD SCHULTZ

A brand is a living, breathing thing and will undoubtedly evolve as your product adds features or as the marketplace changes. That can make it hard for an entrepreneur to decide when to declare yourself "done" with brand development and ready to bring that brand to market. You can start by making sure "there's a level of rigor . . . in the beginning," says Emily Heyward, co-founder of branding agency Red Antler, which has counted companies like Casper and Birchbox as clients.

That rigor starts by being crystal-clear on what your company stands for. Begin with that one-sentence description of what your product is or what your company does—the elevator pitch you've likely practiced and maybe even mastered. But when it comes to your brand, Heyward says that's not nearly enough. You need to address three other questions: What is the purpose of your company? How is your company going to connect with people? And why should people care?

The answers you come up with shouldn't feel flip or dismissive. They should feel like a part of you, and a part of each and every one of your people, inside of each and every function within your company. If you can't articulate those answers, if everyone in your organization can't articulate them clearly, not only do you not know what your brand is, but you're simply not ready to go to market, Heyward says.

Once you've answered those questions, you need to make sure the brand you've uncovered is viable for the long term—you need to future-proof it. You can do that, says John Cinquina, the founder of brand strategy agency Red Meets Blue Branding, and author of *Build Great Brands*, by periodically holding a strategic meeting with your organization's key stakeholders to clarify the plan for the coming twelve months, as well as three, five, and ten years out. Consider the markets you might operate in, the size you expect to be, your product or service diversification plans, and the opportunities you foresee.

You may have answered these in the past, but this time, discuss these variables within the context of your brand. Define what role the brand will play in helping you reach these goals and targets. Brands can only be successfully tied to company growth when you understand what success looks like.

You can go a step further by conducting a touchpoint audit: looking at all of the places a customer or potential customer interacts with your brand. You may see that things have changed since you created a certain type of signage or made a decision, and that it's time to update those manifestations of the brand.

A great brand structured for growth, like most things in a company, should be assessed regularly, Cinquina says. Only you can determine how often you believe that needs to be, but it's worth determining what works for you. This will help inform where to refresh, tweak, and measure. By measuring success, revisiting goals, and discussing improvement strategies, you may find that even small tweaks can go a long way. For some, that means quarterly, for others annually.

THE BRAND OF "YOU"

" For better or for worse, our company is a reflection of my thinking, my character, and my values."

RUPERT MURDOCH

Now your company has a brand. But should you? Many people these days expect to interact with a human—not a faceless company. As a company founder, you *are* the company. So how can you make sure your brand pushes your goals and the company's goals forward?

It's become commonplace these days for entrepreneurs to feel they need a personal brand, but developing a personal brand isn't for everyone. It isn't for introverts, and it isn't for people who can't take a little public criticism—which will happen, inevitably, if you're publishing your opinions.

To cultivate a personal brand that will work in concert with your business brand, there are a few tenets to live by. First, focus on a few of your most-promising market segments, says executive coach, trainer, and consultant Rita B. Allen in her book *Personal Branding and Marketing Yourself*—areas where you can really stand out. You'll get the greatest payoff of your time if you're focused.

Next, know your marketplace and stay a part of it. Stay up to date on your industry, and stay visible within it—becoming a source of information. You should become someone people contact when they want advice or information in a certain area. You can do that through social media, of course, which is critically important for personal brand-building. But don't stop there. Attend networking events and maintain contacts. Keep a database of those contacts.

No matter who you're talking to and in what forum, when it comes to personal brand-building, who you are speaks louder than what you do, says Nicolas Cole, founder of Digital Press, a content marketing and influence agency.

There are a lot of entrepreneurs out there. There are a lot of keynote speakers. There are a lot of marketers, and digital strategists, financial planners, brand executives—and what makes some of them stand out has far more to do with the way they present themselves than whatever it is they "do." You do that through your voice—the distinctive flavor you deliver in speeches or even tweets. You also do that via your style—think Steve Jobs's and Mark Zuckerberg's iconic, oft-discussed sartorial choices. Plus, don't forget your mannerisms. Whether you're the type to maintain unrelenting eye contact or you're a hugger, those choices will become part of your personal brand.

Most important, Cole says, be consistent. Consistency rewards both you and your audience, because it constantly reinforces those elements that comprise your brand. Consistency, Cole says, is how you attract more and more people, for a true following.

It can be tough to keep up. Not to mention addicting: Just ask all those people who obsessively track follows and retweets. A million followers won't make your product great. Don't let your devotion to your own brand come at the expense of what you actually create in the form of your company.

Five Places to Incorporate Your Brand Identity

Your company has spent a lot of time defining and creating your brand and identity. You may have paid a design company to create a logo or a new name and a custom color scheme and paid a web designer to create a website that matched your logo.

But your designer does not define your brand identity. You want that identity to shine through every single day, and become woven into the fabric of your business. Here are five ways to bring your brand into your business, every day, from John Jantsch, author of *Duct Tape Marketing*.

1. **Business Cards.** This seems like an obvious place to start, but some clients and customers will first meet your employees inside or outside the office. Your business cards must not only include your logo and colors, but reflect the quality of your product and your business. Flimsy paper cards, while effective at distributing information, will reflect poorly on your brand.

2. **Emails.** You should create and use a uniform email signature for all employees. This creates immediate credibility for every employee who may have contact with a client with whom they have not previously interacted, and it helps your emails stand out in inboxes.

3. **Workplace.** Regardless of your industry, you will probably have clients and customers in your workspace. Your location and your logo on the wall are not the only things that have an impact on clients. The sounds, smells, and cleanliness of your workplace can also affect their view of your company.

4. **Forms.** A lot of businesses use forms to gather information on their clients and customers. While it may be easy to simply throw something together in order to gather the information needed, it is worth it to spend some time designing the forms so they fit with your logo and branding. This goes for online forms, too.

5. **Talking Points.** Everyone knows the importance of great customer service. Bad customer service often results in bad reviews and negative referrals. But sometimes, a small component of your customer service can be what makes you stand out. For instance, Gates, a popular BBQ restaurant in Kansas City, has their employees ask, "Hi, may I help you?"

to every one of their customers. While this seems standard, their cashiers are so consistent about doing this that it has become a part of their brand. Their logo now proudly features the phrase "Hi, may I help you?". Their business became so well known for something so simple that it became a major part of their brand.

———————

3

POSITIONING YOUR PRODUCT

WE GO THROUGH OUR lives classifying things in our minds and categorizing them in relation to other, similar things. Cars, political candidates, even (maybe especially) dates. It's human nature to subconsciously classify the things we encounter every day.

That's why defining your product's position in the category it occupies—and how it's different from that of your competitors—is critical. If you position your product well in the minds of your customers, that's half the battle of getting them to think of your company when they're ready to buy, says Jay Steinfeld, founder and CEO of Blinds.com.

Effective product positioning involves not only how and where you advertise, but also what you say. In the crowded, price-driven blinds business, for example, almost every seller claims it's the cheapest, Steinfeld notes. Yet, most of the time price alone isn't enough reason for customers to choose one blind company over another.

That's why Blinds.com positioned themselves differently, Steinfeld says. Building on a belief that most people are more concerned about screwing up and choosing blinds that either make their homes look horrible or make themselves look like idiots for having chosen them—or both—they carved out a niche for themselves by offering online design consulting in addition to selling blinds. That positioning helps them stand out from big box stores and other competition.

FIND YOUR TARGET

With a clearly defined target audience, it is much easier to determine where and how to market your company. You can start by looking at your current customer base (if you already have customers). Why do your customers buy from you—do they have common characteristics and interests? It is very likely that other people like them could also benefit from your product or service.

On the flip side, check out who your competitors are targeting. Who are their current customers? Don't go after the same market. You may find a niche market that they are overlooking.

Once you have a general idea of who you're already talking to and the crowded space you might want to avoid, write out a list of each feature of your product or service. Next to each feature, list the benefits it provides (and the benefits of those benefits). For example, a graphic designer offers high-quality design services. The benefit is a professional company image. A professional image will attract more customers because they see the company as professional and trustworthy. So ultimately, the benefit of high-quality design is gaining more customers and making more money.

Once you have your benefits listed, make a list of people who have a need that your benefit fulfills. For example, a graphic designer could choose to target businesses interested in increasing her client base. While this is still too general, you now have a base to start from.

GET SPECIFIC

Figure out not only who has a need for your product or service, but also who is most likely to buy it. Think about the following factors:

→ Age

→ Location

→ Gender

→ Income level

→ Education level

→ Marital or family status

→ Occupation

→ Ethnic background

CONSIDER PSYCHOGRAPHICS

Psychographics are the more personal characteristics of a person, including:

→ Personality

→ Attitudes

→ Values

→ Interests and hobbies

→ Lifestyle

→ Behavior

Psychographics help you figure out how your product or service will fit into your target's lifestyle. How and when will your target use the product? What features are most appealing to your target? What media does your target turn to for information? Does your target read the newspaper, search online, or attend particular events? Who, or what, influences them?

———

Want an example of strong product positioning? Take a look at Harley-Davidson. Here's the company's internal positioning statement:

THE ONLY MOTORCYCLE MANUFACTURER

THAT MAKES BIG, LOUD MOTORCYCLES

FOR MACHO GUYS (AND "MACHO WANNABES")

MOSTLY IN THE UNITED STATES

WHO WANT TO JOIN A GANG OF COWBOYS

IN AN ERA OF DECREASING PERSONAL FREEDOM.

———

EVALUATE YOUR DECISION

Once you've decided on a target market, be sure to consider these questions:

→ Are there enough people who fit my criteria?

→ Will my target really benefit from my product/service? Will they see a need for it?

→ Do I understand what drives my target to make decisions?

→ Can they afford my product/service?

→ Can I reach them with my message? Are they easily accessible?

Don't break your target down too far. Remember, you can have more than one niche market. Consider if your marketing message should be different for each niche. If you can reach both niches effectively with the same message, then maybe you have broken down your market too far. Also, if you find there are only fifty people that fit all of your criteria, maybe you should reevaluate your target. The trick is to find that perfect balance.

You may be asking, "How do I find all this information?" Try searching online for research others have done on your target. Search for articles that talk about or to your target market. Search for blogs and forums where people in your target market communicate their opinions. Look for survey results, or consider conducting a survey of your own. Ask your current customers for feedback.

Once you have all of the information, you can break it down this way to come up with a simplified positioning statement:

For (target customer)

Who (statement of need or opportunity),

(Product name) is a (product category)

That (statement of key benefit).

Unlike (competing alternative)

(Product name) (statement of primary differentiation).

Defining your target market is the hard part. Once you know who you are targeting, it is much easier to figure out which media you can use to reach them and what marketing messages will resonate with them. Instead of sending direct mail to everyone in your ZIP code, only send it to those who fit your criteria. Save money and get a better return on investment by defining your target audience.

Five Tips to Writing an Effective Mission Statement

 Once you determine who you're talking to, it's time to get deeper.

Knowing your customers inside and out isn't a new philosophy; marketing greats have preached it for decades. But the way you collect and synthesize that information has evolved. And this is not a one-and-done process. Staying in tune with your customer has to be ongoing and iterative.

1. Developing personas is a good place to start when trying to get inside your customer's head, says Jeff Pruitt, CEO of strategy, branding, and design company Tallwave. If you have customers already, start getting conversations going with them.

2. Don't limit this to just your most loyal customers, either. For the most accurate data, you'll want to canvass a real cross-section of customers: the net promoter or raving fan; the power-user who always provides quality, actionable feedback to the dev team; the mature, fully implemented customer who doesn't say much, but will likely never leave; and even those who, let's face it, aren't all that happy with your brand. Describe those people in as much detail as possible.

3. It's also important to note that the customers you either lose after a sale or during the sales process can provide valuable information as well. There's a reason they're leaving, and a reason they're picking another company or product. This insight will tell you a lot about your ideal customer profile.

4. The more of this information you can gather directly from the customer, the better. Even if you don't have all of the answers, fill in as many blanks as you can. You want this persona to be as real in your mind—and your sales team's mind—as possible.

5. If you don't have customers yet, get out there and talk to as many people as you can who are willing. More important than the number is to actually listen, and try to understand where customers and potential customers are coming from. Rational or emotional, the buying decision often comes down to a gut feeling—if you can capture that, you're well on your way.

———

HOW MUCH SHOULD YOU SPEND?

DEPENDING ON YOUR POINT of view, marketing can either seem like a waste of money, or an essential expense that can generate much-needed revenue. Both perspectives can be right. In large part, finding your company's spending sweet spot will depend on how effective your marketing is.

While you may encounter times you're willing to spend more—during a product launch, for example—and other times when you need to rein it in, knowing a few basic numbers can give you a helpful perspective to frame your marketing spend.

It helps to start with your customer acquisition cost (CAC). That's the average cost of acquiring a new customer. Determining your CAC is easy: Add up all your sales and marketing costs for a specific period of time and then divide by the number of new customers landed during that period.

If you spend $100 and acquire 10 customers, your CAC is $10.

What's a good number? That's harder to answer. It really depends on your industry and business model. It's also important to understand how CAC fits into your overall operating budget. The leaner your operation overall, the more you can afford to spend to acquire a customer. Plus, the longer you hang onto customers in general, the more you can justify on each new customer acquisition. That's a customer's lifetime value, or LTV, which can be defined as the profit your company can expect to generate from a customer, multiplied by the typical amount of time you hang onto the customer (e.g., x number of years).

Once you've built a little history you can start to spot customer retention and spending trends. Then the math gets a lot easier: Determine what the average customer spends over a specific time period and calculate the return on your original customer acquisition cost investment.

There's more you can learn from tracking. A rising CAC means you'll need to start cutting costs or raising prices—or do a better job in marketing and sales. A falling LTV can be more troubling: It means you may need to spend more on marketing, but it also indicates that you're failing to leverage the most important and least expensive customers you have: current ones.

MARKETING ON A LIMITED BUDGET

As a startup, you walk a fine line with your marketing spend. We're telling you that you won't succeed unless consumers know your products and services exist (which takes a heavy marketing and advertising investment). But let's be real—you probably don't have a large budget, and spending too much on a launch campaign can doom you from the start. The trick is to find that sweet spot that should allow you to reach a large audience with a conservative budget.

Over the years, that sweet spot has changed—and it's different for each industry and type of business—but the concept remains the same. Word-of-mouth marketing has always been a startup's best chance of success when working with a limited budget. The Internet has only intensified that trend, and accelerated the way that word of mouth travels.

Social media has made it possible for small startup businesses to reach millions of consumers with the click of a button: Just consider the fact that adults now spend five and a half hours a week on social media, and just under half (45 percent) of U.S. adults use Facebook for news.[1]

So your customers are out there on social media, no doubt. And they're in other places, too—commuting via subway, showing up at key conferences, or pushing their kids in swings at the park. You just need to find them, and connect with them. That's what this book will help you do.

But before selecting which channels you'll use, you need a detailed strategy that will drive your focus, determine where to allocate your funds, and keep you on track.

Here are the steps that you can take to get started.

DEFINE YOUR IDEAL CUSTOMER PROFILE

Before you spend a dime on marketing, take the time to research your audience. It's the most important part of your marketing strategy, and it comes before the development of any campaign. Without research, you'll never know where to focus your marketing efforts. You'll end up with a poor return, regardless of whether you spend $1,000 or $100,000.

Research takes a lot of forms and should include, at minimum, the following:

- → Identifying your target audience (you've already done this)

- → Audience segmentation (how different members of your audience should or could be targeted). Your personas should help here.

- → Competitive analysis

- → Customer surveys

- → Audience pain points in relation to your product or service

This research serves as the foundation for every campaign you create for pre- and post-launch efforts. Yes, you can buy data reports for your audience or industry. But it's often not necessary, since you can uncover almost all of this information with a little judicious digging.

IDENTIFY WHAT MAKES THEM TICK

Once you've spent time discovering your ideal customer segment, figure out the platforms that they hang out on, given their specific interests. Find out where they go to consume content—is it blogs, YouTube, Snapchat, or Instagram? Do they watch TV or read certain trade publications?

A good path for discovery would be to speak to some of your potential customers in and around you. Ask them their preferred platforms and what they do on each social media channel they're frequenting. Ask them what they read, and why. This will help you prioritize. (You're not going to try to be on all of the channels at once—more on that later.)

IDENTIFY THE FORMAT AND MESSAGING

Once you know the channels, you have a better understanding of the format the content will need to take. For instance, if you're looking at Snapchat and YouTube, you pretty much know it's going to be delivered via video.

On the other hand, if Facebook and Instagram are the channels you want to focus on, you will have multiple format options. You could make videos, articles, images, or some of each. Your strategy will be different if your audience commutes via subway every day, staring at advertising posters.

While you're deciding on the content format and the go-to channel(s), it's important to have specific strategies for each channel. Posting the same content across all social media channels is not going to get you the desired result because people interact with different channels differently. Choose one or two channels that you believe will most effectively reach your potential audience, and then format your messaging and craft content to fit the chosen channel or channels.

DETERMINE YOUR PRIMARY GOALS

After homing in on where your audience is, define your goals. While many large, established corporations use marketing across channels to facilitate growth in all areas of business, it's more likely that a startup will focus on one or two of the following:

→ **Brand awareness.** Just about every startup these days uses social media for driving brand awareness. It happens organically as you post content, engage with users, and promote your brand.

While it can be done cheaply and quickly, as more brands populate social channels, a clear strategy is increasingly required to cut through the clutter.

→ **Content distribution.** Many brands and businesses use social media as a content distribution and dissemination platform. If your content is engaging and unique enough, it's possible that others could share your posts and advertise your brand for you.

→ **Lead generation.** Ideally, you would like your marketing to drive traffic to your website or blog. This requires a long-term investment and results usually aren't seen for many months.

→ **Customer acquisition.** Finally, the best-case scenario is that your marketing raises brand awareness, your content generates leads, and leads turn into customers.

CHOOSE YOUR CHANNELS

Depending on your strategy, approach, and goals, you should be able to determine which platforms or channels are right for your startup. We dive into that in detail in the next section of the book.

Social media isn't the only cheap option (and it's not always cheap, as you'll see in the next section of this book). Some startups have great success thinking offline. For example, you can set up a free meetup for potential customers (using space you already have, and serving bagels and coffee), and use the attendee information to offer white papers, newsletters, or other content. You can guest-post on another company's blog. It's a great way to drive traffic to your site.

You could also leverage another company's prospect or customer list in exchange for giving free product to people on the list, or via some kind of cross-promotional agreement. If you have a new kind of toothbrush, for example, reach out to dentists in your area.

> " In ed-tech, our buyers read email before 7:00 a.m. or after 3:30 p.m. and if we are going to do a webinar, then it needs to be between 7:00 p.m. and 8:00 p.m. Knowing when your potential buyer is engaged in content is critical to the success of your marketing plans."

KATHARINE MOBLEY, CMO, Crescerance

ONLINE MARKETING

SEO

What you knew about search engine optimization—or thought you knew—just a few years ago is likely different today.

It's been years since you could game Google's rankings with clever meta-tagging, simple keyword inputs, and the production of lots of similar content. Today, the algorithm is more sophisticated, with protections built in to prevent spam and content farms from showing up at the top of rankings. Many businesses have caught on to that. More than ever, the content that's ranked highly is created by humans for humans—and that's obvious when you see it.

Marketers must also keep up with the changing nature of how consumers search. In contrast to a few years ago, today's searchers are using search strings of five or six words—think phrases or sentence fragments—to get the results they want. While keyword tracking is still a part of today's SEO, the focus on ranking for shorter, more general keywords is all but gone. Large organizations with huge budgets may still be able to rank for those terms, but most businesses have realized that this strategy is extremely expensive—not to mention ineffective.

Customers are also thinking local, because of Google's habit of providing personalized search results. This means that two people can search for entirely the same thing, but get two sets of results based on their geographical location.

To take advantage of these shifts, think less about specific keywords and instead focus on writing longform content that naturally ranks for those long-tail search queries. For instance, ranking for "windows" may make you feel pretty important in the window installation industry, but likely won't result in high conversion rates. Ranking for "double-hung window installation San Francisco," on the other hand, is far more likely to result in sales. You'll know where to start for your industry, and Google Analytics will help you narrow it down—try inputting different combinations of words and phrases and research related terms, too.

SEO requires a commitment over the long term; it's not a quick fix. As a start, experts recommend focusing on content formats that earn links, like longform, research-based articles, opinion-forming features, or comprehensive explainer and list posts because they provide more depth for search. When coming up with new topics for your content, keyword research can be invaluable. It gives you insight into the words and phrases people use to find your products or services, enabling you to create content that people are actually looking for.

Once work on a particular SEO initiative has been completed, it takes time to see optimal results. Search engines need to find and index new content; competitors are constantly changing their tactics—meaning you may also need to change yours before you see results; and it often takes time to build traction for new content in the form of inbound links and social shares—both of which will help boost your ranking.

How Measurable Is It?

If you're just measuring page views (or likes, or followers) who come in through search, you're probably not going far enough, says Dave Kerpen, CEO of Likeable Local. Vanity metrics like those offer a narrow window into a website's effectiveness. After all, a million site visitors aren't going to help you if none of them are converting. Google Analytics can help you dig a little deeper into the numbers to start collecting more actionable data. Here are a few data points to start with:

→ **Customized metrics.** Even if your page views are through the roof, that number alone doesn't give you enough information to take a certain action. Conversion rate is a much more important metric to track. Bounce rate is another easy statistic to find, but bounce rate by source can indicate how well-qualified your traffic is from an individual source. Determine where you need more information from your analytics. Custom reports can show you the unique data your company needs. For example, analyze traffic and behavior to show where customers come from and what they do when they get to your website.

→ **ROI calculation.** Stop crossing your fingers. ROI calculation takes a few steps to set up in Google Analytics, but the payoff is huge. Setting values to your goals will show you which customer actions result in the most revenue. Once you know that, you can optimize your page with ROI in mind.

→ **Source attribution.** Search marketing doesn't live within a vacuum. A customer might check you out initially from organic search, come back later via a Twitter post, and make a purchase from an email. If you only track the customer's last interaction, you won't be attributing accurate value to your social or SEO presence. Attribution models can reveal which sources lead to conversions. This can help you predict which initiatives will be successful in the future.

→ **Visitor behavior.** Users Flow reports depict the paths that visitors take through your website. Understanding these paths can help you streamline your conversion process and reduce friction. If you have a lot of drop-offs at your shopping cart, you could offer a coupon code to the visitor in exchange for filling out the form. Just like that, you've captured their information and have an opportunity to nurture the relationship.

→ **Conversion goals.** What do you want people to do after they come to your site? Downloading white papers or subscribing to an email newsletter is great, but how do you assign a dollar amount to those actions? Google Analytics allows you to assign goal values to specific actions. When you calculate values for customer actions, you can prove the success of your campaigns.

 ## How Much Does It Cost?

Like so many marketing disciplines, there's a range. A self-taught freelancer may charge $75 an hour to audit your content, perform keyword analysis, and develop a link-building strategy so your site generates important third-party links to it. More established firms may charge closer to $200 an hour, or require an ongoing contract or per-project pricing. A monthly, contract, or project plan may allow you to take a more holistic view of the work, rather than counting hours and stressing out if they begin to tip past your budget limit.

Can I DIY?

Search engine optimization should have a place in every company's marketing arsenal, but staying abreast of SEO's evolutionary leaps isn't simple. Yes, you can mine Google Analytics as a starting point, and attempt to craft your content and site accordingly, but an expert vendor can up your game materially. It's no longer good enough to just be noticed online. You have to be noticed by the right people at the right time with the right content.

It's the quick shifts in this landscape that make it a tough bet for effective do-it-yourselfing. Google has been known to make sudden, significant changes that render large parts of an SEO strategy obsolete. As an example, the company has said that mobile-first content indexing is coming—meaning sites will be ranked according to how well they cater to the mobile user. When that happens, it's likely to mean significant changes to algorithms and, as a result, SEO strategies.

Tapping the vast network of available marketing resources and outsourcing choices may seem like a letdown to founders with DIY on the brain. But from a pragmatic standpoint, letting professionals work their magic often makes more sense than risking a sloppy job that has to be redone—particularly because compared with other marketing initiatives, this one doesn't need to set you back tens of thousands of dollars when you outsource to a pro.

EMAIL

Email marketing has two massive benefits: It can be done quite cheaply, and it's incredibly easy to measure. Taken together, it's easy to understand why email has become the first type of marketing many companies take on, and the one they focus on most.

Email offers other benefits to marketers as well. Aside from delivering great metrics, it delivers a regular way of staying in front of your customers, whether you're offering an ongoing newsletter or a promotion. Email can be used by your business to market to customers, alert them to new product offerings, and offer loyalty discounts or promotions. At the same time, your customers can use email to troubleshoot any problems they have with your products or services, provide you feedback, and ask questions.

But email campaigns—often hailed as the reigning ROI champions of digital marketing—only work if they have an audience. That's an increasing challenge in an era where consumers are bombarded with email marketing messages. For most companies, the greatest challenge in email marketing is building a targeted list with accurate information. An urban apartment dweller doesn't want content about landscaping, and a mom of three probably isn't interested in late-night entertainment. Accurate targeting and segmenting is critical to your success.

Email marketing is part art and part science. It takes a combination of know-how and creativity to get customers and clients just to open your email—let alone to read the whole thing, or click through to your site.

What's Your Subject?

Your subject line is the headline for your email. Numerous studies have also shown that emails are more likely to be opened if the subject line is two or three words, as opposed to a sentence. Ideally, the teaser—your opening sentences—should complement and reinforce the subject line's relevance.

When you're writing the subject line, avoid gimmicks and tricks. They may work once, but they erode trust and eventually debase most brands. If you're unsure, test it. Actually, even if you *think* you're sure, still test it. A/B testing your subject line is easy: Divide your list in two, each with a different subject line, and track the open rate, click through rate, and purchase/conversion rate on your landing page. This will help you build your best version of sales scripting to use on your website, offline marketing collateral, and even in your live salesperson scripting.

Take extra care with the opening sentences of your message. In most email readers, the Inbox display includes the sender, the time sent, the subject line, and the first twenty words (or so) of the email. Prospects decide whether to open your email based on those four elements, so pack in a benefit to your readers—something they will learn, or get.

Be Real

You want to come across as a real person; your email should come from one specific person, and go to one specific recipient. Don't write to crowds, and don't write from committees or departments or companies. Write to one person. Unless you have a culture that values formality (or work in an industry where that's the norm), start your marketing email with the first name of the prospect, followed by a comma. No honorific (like "Mr.") and no "Dear…". Write as if to a colleague, not your Great Aunt Ruth.

Yes, the email is from your company, but it's not about you. Prospects and customers are interested in themselves, their own careers, their own business, and their own customers (usually in that order). They will shrug off and ignore any message that's primarily about you, your business, your product, your enthusiasm, or your opinion. Make your emails valuable. This can be a key insight, a touching story, a special offer, or anything else that is relevant to your business and your audience. What do you talk with your prospects and customers about when you're with them in person? What do they care about? How do you touch their lives? This is the core of your email messaging.

Whatever you decide as the core of your message, it should be clear and simple. A thread should carry through from your subject line, through the top of the email, to short, skimmable body copy, with mobile-friendly design. Remember, your email is very likely to be opened from someone's phone.

Every email should have a call-to-action—but just one. The more CTAs that you cram in, the less likely it is that the prospect will act. Whether you want someone to click through to your site, to call you, or to respond to a survey depends on the nature of your business.

Before you hit *send*, do a quality assurance check. Test the message on multiple browsers and readers, including on mobile devices and tablets. Check that all of your links work, as well as the landing pages they point to. And don't forget to check spelling and grammar. A simple quality assurance checklist can make sure you've checked everything before you hit the send button.

Test and Test Again

How you send your email is as important as its content. Numerous studies have shown that marketing emails are much more likely to be answered if they are sent when prospects are not juggling all the daily emails that get traded during normal work hours. That assumption, though, depends on your audience. Twenty-something retail shoppers will behave differently than desk-bound mid-career professionals. You can test sending at different times to see what works for your customer base.

Rinse and Repeat for a 46 Percent Open Rate

GERRY BLACK, A MARKETING CONSULTANT and writer, shared with *Inc.* his method for testing email subject lines and increasing open rates.

"Create your email promotion and write out three subject lines. Take your best subject line and include it with your first email. Let's say you email 1,000 people and 150 of them open it. Delete those names off your 'send' list and re-send the email using a different subject line. Once your open results come back from the second email, delete those names and do your third email using your third subject line. You could triple the amount of people who open your email."

Black shared the results from one client's efforts. The first email was sent to 306 recipients, and 84 people opened it. The second email was sent to 222 recipients, and 38 people opened it. The last email was sent to the remainder of the list. Twenty people opened that. Altogether, the same email with different subject lines was sent to 306 people and was opened by 142 people for an open rate of 46 percent.

A cautionary note: You'll need to carefully time *when* you send the emails, with enough time in between. Fail to do that and customers and clients might notice your strategy and be annoyed by the repeat send.

The format that resonates best will also depend on who you're talking to. If most of your audience is opening on a mobile device, focus on short copy and minimal imagery. Test and find your most effective email formats—text vs. HTML, short vs. longform, etc.

Making sure your email gets through—and gets noticed—starts at the very beginning, with your list. It's not the number of email addresses in your list that count; it's the percentage of email addresses belonging to prospects who might buy from you. Think quality over quantity: You want customers or clients who are more likely to purchase your product or service.

The way to get those people is to build your own list. Encourage customers to sign up directly from your website, where they can quickly provide their information and choose exactly what kind of information they want to receive from you. Offer sign-up sheets at your retail counter, conference, workshop, or presentation. If you have a guide or e-book, provide it to anyone who opts in. You want subscribers that want information about your company, product, or service—which makes buying or renting lists a dicey proposition.

Stay on top of your list after each deployment. If your email isn't getting opened, delete that address. Perhaps most important: Offering an opt-out option is essential to not annoy customers and clients, but also as a measure of protecting your brand. You don't want your company emails to be associated with spam.

If you're working with a new list or with a new format or email element, start with a subset of your list first (e.g., your Gmail or Yahoo emails) to make sure there aren't any issues with deliverability or formatting across email clients. This will save you heartache; you don't want emails to 100,000 people to get stopped cold because of something that was easily fixable.

Finally, if an email (or email campaign) was successful, don't be afraid to re-use it. At the very least, re-send it to all those people who didn't open it the first time. And recycle it back to your non-buying prospects a second and third time down the road after some time has passed.

How Much Does It Cost?

Firing off an email costs nothing—but that's probably not how you'll want to execute your email marketing. Basic email marketing services from reliable vendors are almost always free up to a point—possibly a couple of thousand contacts or a certain number of emails deployed each month. At that point, you'll pay a monthly fee of $100 or more, depending on the size of your send as well as bells and whistles like time zone-specific sending and extensive testing and reporting.

When you're considering providers—and there are dozens—balance complexity with power. There is a cost to switching platforms that is many times the cost of the service. Choose wisely and don't be lured by features you're unlikely to use. Mail Chimp and Constant Contact are popular options, as are the more robust vendors Infusionsoft or Hubspot, which go way beyond basic email sends and have broader marketing capabilities (see Chapter 12 for more on marketing software).

Can I DIY?

Absolutely. Choose a software provider that offers design options that make sense for your business, and don't underestimate the power of professional copywriting, if you can afford it. It may also be worth upgrading to a software package that includes technical support, so you don't waste your valuable time trying to troubleshoot if you run into hiccups.

How Measurable Is It?

Data junkies love email marketing. You can see who opens your email, which links are being clicked, who forwarded your email, bounce rates, and how many (and which) readers unsubscribed. Many software services will serve up this data for you in the form of post-send reports. A few metrics to start with: First, test your open rate using different combinations of the subject line and the first fifteen words. Second, test for response rate using variations of yes/no questions. Finally, test for conversion rate by tracking which responses turn into purchases.

SOCIAL MEDIA MARKETING

Here's what we know: Social media marketing is essential. Your customers are out there, connecting with peers, influencers, and brands.

But here's what we don't know: What's next, and what's on its way out. Social media moves incredibly fast. Brands can only react: Audiences control the medium while brands merely ride the wave until the next new channel comes along.

Successful brands have to evolve with their audience and platforms. Too many marketers, at companies big and small, have thrown money at social media marketing without knowing the "why" behind their strategy. Like any part of your marketing arsenal, you should consider social as one arm of a larger strategy. Forrester puts it best when they say that you don't need a "social marketing" strategy; you need marketing that uses social tactics and technology strategically alongside other channels to achieve your goals.[1]

So how do you know where to put your scarce resources? Like so many marketing channels, it comes down to knowing your audience inside and out. You need to "think about where their audiences are, what they are reading, what they are doing," says Kenneth Hitchner, public relations and social media director for Creative Marketing Alliance. "If you are marketing to seniors, you're not going to be using the latest social media app like Snapchat because the audience isn't there—just like if you are marketing to teens you probably aren't going to use something like LinkedIn." It's impossible to be omnipresent: Your brand's social media strategy should be centered on the platforms where your target audience is spending the most time, so you're not competing in a sea of noise.

One of the biggest early stage mistakes is to spread yourself out across multiple social networks. Instead, find out where your audience is hanging out and be there. Then master those two to three networks. Show up consistently and engage in conversation.

Once you've identified the right channels (we break that down for you next), consider the balance between paid marketing and organic reach—that is, the impression you get when someone comes directly to your page, not by clicking an ad. Organic visitors sought you out; they're more highly qualified and more likely to buy. Great social content can be incredibly effective in generating that all-important organic reach, particularly when it's coupled with a strategic media spend.

For example, says serial entrepreneur and famed social media strategist Gary Vaynerchuk, if you just start using the proper hashtags on Instagram, you can easily start being discovered over time. Whether you're a local pizza shop or a car dealership, or an artist, or a Fortune 500 B2B company, using hashtags is an organic way to hit discoverability and create amplification for your content. And if you have paid media dollars, even just spending $100 to $300 a week on the amplification of your YouTube and Facebook video content can make your content explode, he adds—as long as that content is high quality to begin with.

Next: Uncover the kind of content that works best in each channel—and how they all fit together as part of a larger strategy.

Facebook

Companies using Facebook to reach their target audience used to have it easy. No more. Today, the world's largest social network is teeming with companies and influencers vying for attention. But you don't have to be huge or deep-pocketed to succeed on Facebook, the behemoth of social media platforms.

As an entrepreneur with a limited budget and resources, it may seem like a fool's errand to try and compete against massive companies with seemingly bottomless pockets. It's not. Regardless of your budget, the market responds to brands that offer value—and that value comes in the form of great, relevant content.

One of the most important things that you can do with regard to Facebook marketing success is to create content with the goal of developing a community, says Neil Patel, co-founder of web analytics firm CrazyEgg. Start with unpaid posts. Write content that provokes conversation. If you do this, you will increase audience engagement and increase the odds of your content getting shared. Most content marketers today try to shoot for the moon with every piece of content, creating mountains of work and lots of stress.

To create great, relevant content, start by looking at what's already working for other companies—both in your industry and out—and model their success. Depending on what you do, that may mean how-to articles, quick tips, or conversation starters. A yoga studio with a professional clientele, for example, may post tips about proper posture at work. A meal service company may post recipes. A software company may post articles about customer relationship management.

Once you have started creating high-quality content on a consistent basis, the next step is to use that content as a springboard to build a community, Patel says. You want your content to convey that you truly understand your audience. It should be audience first; meaning, you're publishing content your audience needs—not pushing out things that are linked to your latest product launch or campaign. If your audience truly finds your content helpful, they will start to promote your content for you through sharing. That's far better than any sort of paid advertising you could do on your own, and it's free.

As you post content, track and analyze it. Find the weak spots in your arsenal as well as the strengths you didn't know you had. Facebook Insights can help you here. Using that tool, you can see:

→ How many shares are you generating for each type of post?

→ What sort of posts generate more engagement?

→ Are you reaching the conversion rates you thought you would?

The data doesn't lie, so don't make excuses for your underperforming content. Once you answer these questions, you'll see the changes you need to make.

Paying for More

Is it worth taking it a step further and paying for Facebook advertising? That depends on your goals. Facebook is increasingly powerful for geo-targeted ads. It's also a gathering place for audiences that belong to a certain niche on the Internet, or with a self-identified interest. You can focus on defining characteristics of your ideal customers, including their likes and interests, the pages they follow, the apps they use, and more. You will need to do some research and look for individual publications and blogs your ideal customer will likely follow and use this insight to focus in on what pages your customers likely follow. This is one of the most effective ways to ensure your ads are getting to the right people.

Remember that people use Facebook for sharing content, not for consuming ads. If you want your ads to be effective and to stand out, they need to be as valuable, or even more valuable, than the other content being presented in people's feeds.

Thinking in those terms will help you figure out how to frame your posts—but many business owners simply don't know how to provide value. Many of them fear giving away too much for free. Or they worry that if they don't use a sales-driven headline that nobody will click. But you have to remember where you are running ads—your users are not primed for sales content. You need to act accordingly.

Once you start running ads, don't cheer (or freak out) too quickly. It's common to experience anxiety once you kick off an ad campaign and you can see the dollars draining in real time. Facebook ads take time to refine and adjust in order to work properly. You can't run a campaign for a day and immediately chalk it up as a failure—especially if you're first starting out.

Once the data come in and you're ready to make changes, tweak element by element. Leave most things in place, as constants—just tweak one or two variables at a time. Otherwise you'll never know if it was the headline that made the difference, or the image, or the offer. Seemingly tiny things, like changing "daily tips" to "pro tips" in your copy, can make a marked difference, so don't overlook the details of your text and imagery.

The key to creating a successful campaign—without wasting tons of money—is to test before you scale. You have to keep testing until you have found the right audience, ad creative, and landing page that has optimal conversions. When executed adeptly, Facebook advertising is one of the most powerful platforms for paid traffic.

 ## How Much Does It Cost?

In theory, an amount as small as $100 can get your message in front of 1,000 people or more. But that doesn't mean they're the right 1,000 people.

When you set up your campaign, you can set a cap on your spend. Many experienced advertisers recommend capping your spend at $50 or $100 a week and tweaking along the way. Targeting tightly on certain geographic areas, interests, or other options will help you make sure you're not driving up your costs with lots of useless clicks. According to WordStream, the average click through rate (CTR) across all industries is 0.9 percent, with an average cost per click of $1.72.[2] But the numbers can vary dramatically by industry.

Make sure you consider the cost of ongoing testing. Split-testing doesn't just take time, it also costs money. That's why you need an ad budget that includes a line item for split-testing.

Too many marketers make the mistake of budgeting money for running an ad, but never for the testing period. As a result, they eat into their advertising budget when they conduct experiments. That leaves them with less money than they should have for the actual campaign.

How Measurable Is It?

You can measure virtually every aspect of a Facebook marketing campaign, and you should. Just make sure you're looking at the right metrics to truly measure efficacy.

Consider this example:

During a recent testing period, you noticed that Campaign A sent ten people to your site whereas Campaign B only sent three people.

Easy decision. Campaign A is the winner, right?

Maybe not. You just measured leads in that test, not conversions.

Suppose only one in ten visitors from Campaign A makes a purchase, but two out of three visitors from Campaign B makes a purchase. Which campaign is the winner in that case?

The campaign that gives you the most conversions, but not necessarily the most leads, is the one you want to invest in.

The lesson here is not to get manipulated by vanity metrics. You need to have a clear understanding of what it is that you want to accomplish with your ads. Make sure that you write these goals down as they can govern the decisions you make with your ads. Do you want new customers? How many? Do you want more visits to your website? Are you looking to get people to register for your event? The more specific you are with your goals, the more you can tailor your ads to help you reach your goals, and the more you can track your progress to make necessary tweaks to your ads.

Can I DIY?

Absolutely. Setting up a Facebook ad campaign is straightforward, and you can easily cap your spend so it doesn't run away from you. One of the problems people run into when they DIY is that they don't have the expertise to know about all of the advertising-related tools Facebook offers.

Make sure you use Facebook's built-in tools to:

→ **Boost Your Posts.** Remember when you post an update on Facebook, only a fraction of your fans will see it. If you promote your post, it will extend its reach.

→ **Promote Your Page.** If your goal with your Facebook advertisements is to grow your Facebook page, then you need to use the Promote Your Page feature. Facebook gives you the option to test different images and add a call to action to your posts if you utilize this feature.

→ **Send People to Your Website.** If your ultimate goal is about getting more people to your website, then you can utilize this feature, designed specifically to help drive traffic to your site.

And, as we said earlier, make sure to target tightly, cap your weekly spend, and learn and evolve as you go.

LINKEDIN

Unless you work in consulting or B2B services, LinkedIn may not be top-of-mind as you consider your marketing strategy. But the networking site offers lots of low-investment ways to raise your profile, no matter what you do.

First, you should know that anything you post on the site is viewable for anyone on the web to find or see via Google search, which hasn't always been the case. That means your profile as well as every piece of content you publish on LinkedIn is "public" (unless you change your user settings). You want to be "found" online, and this adds even more SEO juice to your content efforts on LinkedIn.

When a potential customer, supplier, or partner finds you online, having a polished LinkedIn presence is one way to boost your start-up's credibility.

Start with Your Profile

The first thing you need to do is build a LinkedIn profile and comprehensive company page, says marketing expert Samuel Edwards. Playing around with an individual profile allows you to familiarize yourself with the functions of the site. If potential customers are going to stumble onto your profile—and they likely will—make sure it's polished. A few basics to include:

→ **A professional image.** Profiles without pictures are rarely viewed, while those with high-quality images are perceived as much more professional. It's best to include a solid white or colored background, wear professional dress, and smile. You want to come off as being sophisticated, yet personable. It doesn't need to be a professional head shot, but it should look polished.

→ **A descriptive headline.** LinkedIn allows you to customize your "Professional Headline," and you'll want to spend some time crafting it. For example, instead of simply putting "Marketing Professional," something along the lines of "Founder of marketing automation software company, Zippy" is much more compelling.

→ **Relevant work history.** The meat of your profile will consist of your work history and resume. While you don't want to leave off important jobs you've held, you also should avoid including things that are irrelevant—like part-time high school summer jobs or memberships in college clubs and societies. Rather than treating your LinkedIn profile as an autobiography of your working life, treat it as a way to show why your experience makes you a credible supplier of whatever you're selling.

→ **A custom URL.** LinkedIn gives you the ability to customize your URL. Try using something that's simple, short, and is associated with your name. If first and last name aren't available, consider incorporating initials or abbreviations.

After using LinkedIn as an individual user, you can begin to delve into the business features by creating a company page. As with your individual profile, there are some specific tips and tricks to mastering your company page.

→ **A compelling summary.** This is the most important part of your company page. The summary appears right under your cover image and allows you to explain who you are, what you do, and why readers should believe in you. While the summary needs to include basic information about the company and what you do, it should also be descriptive, conversational, and engaging. Many entrepreneurs tend to think from the inside out: This is our product, here are its features. Instead, think from the outside in, and audience first: Our customers buy from us in order to achieve this goal, or we're solving this problem.

→ **A compelling image.** While the summary may be the most important aspect, your image has the ability to ruin your profile from the start. Make sure the image represents everything your brand stands for and is high quality and unique. This isn't a place to use stale stock photos; invest in something original.

→ **Accurate contact info.** Double-check to ensure all fields are complete and accurate. You won't be able to generate any leads unless you get this information right.

Once you have your own individual profile and a company page, you're ready to start generating leads for your business. The first step is simply to connect. LinkedIn is a social network, so get social. Build a list of every single person that you may want to do business with in the future. This list could include investors, clients, and other potential partners. Once the list is done, go through one by one and add them to your network. Include a custom and highly personalized note for each person and begin to send requests. Your entire goal here is to expand your network with people you want to know you exist. As your network grows, you now have a highly focused and targeted list of people that will receive a notification every time you post content.

Now that you've built up your connections, you're ready to start creating content. Content shows up in online searches as well as appearing in your contacts' feeds.

If you're already producing content, LinkedIn is a great way to spread it to a wider audience. If you already blog, for instance, you can get extra mileage from each post by posting a link to the post on LinkedIn, and then publishing the full version a few days later.

LinkedIn makes it very easy to produce content via the "write an article" button on your home page. Every time you post something, a notification goes out to all your connections. This means that every piece of carefully crafted content can potentially end up in front of anyone that you are connected with on LinkedIn.

Another free way to get noticed is by joining LinkedIn groups. Social media is a two-way street. You can't simply push content on people and expect them to respond. The best way to give back to your users is to join groups and become an active member by providing advice, answering questions, and building one-on-one relationships. In return, your activity in these groups will increase your exposure and possibly position you as a thought leader in your niche.

The great thing about LinkedIn groups is that people have self-selected (or have been invited) to be a part of a targeted community, notes Janine Popick, co-founder of business data dashboard Dasheroo. And there are literally millions of them. The community is made up of people who like to share their content, get a job description out there (or look at some), and network with like-minded pros.

If that community is based around an industry you serve, you need to be a part of it.

It's simple: In LinkedIn's search bar, type in the keywords that match your industry. Then assess all of the groups that surface that you want to be a member of. It's important to make sure you fill out your LinkedIn profile and company profile as much as possible. LinkedIn will go ahead and recommend groups for you to join.

Once you join, make sure you check in every so often, participate in the discussion, and share updates you think the group might be interested in—it essentially amounts to free advertising. And when someone replies to your updates, make sure you acknowledge with his name in your own reply to clearly indicate that you've read what he said.

 ## Can I DIY?

Definitely. LinkedIn is all about personal connections—your content would feel awkward if it appeared to be written by someone else.

It never hurts, though, to get professional editorial eyes on all of your content, including your profile, your company page, and the articles you post.

How Much Does It Cost?

So far, everything we've talked about is free. If you want to get your content in front of even more eyeballs, try sponsored updates, available through LinkedIn's "Campaign Manager" tool. It allows companies to push their content to the top of people's feeds as well as offering targeting by gender, age, location, group membership, company, and a host of other options. It operates on a pay-per-click or pay-per-1000 impressions model (if you care more about how many times the ad is shown rather than clicked on). The minimum costs are extremely low—as little as $10 per day.

How Measurable Is It?

It depends. It's tough to measure the ongoing conversations that LinkedIn may generate. But the moment you make a big sale from a connection you forged, you'll be glad you put in the time.

If you're posting content with links back to your site, you'll be able to measure referral traffic, targeted page views, and lifts in subscribers or opt-ins. If you're employing paid content or LinkedIn ads, you have more tools at your disposal; through LinkedIn's Campaign Manager, you'll see your engagement rate, which tracks clicks, shares, and comments.

TWITTER

Twitter is about getting out there: generating followers and participating in conversations. It's not an overnight strategy—it takes time and patience to cultivate connections, participate in conversations, and generate followers and retweets. "Twitter is a cocktail party," says social media strategist Vaynerchuk. "How do you become really good at a cocktail party? You show up, you go into a circle, you start talking," he says. "If you are a listener and you actually add something to the conversation, we become friends."

You may be tempted to jump in and offer up your service right away or to ask for endorsements. Don't. Be patient and deliver value; listen before you tweet. You wouldn't walk into a real cocktail party and start shouting or ask other people to tell everyone that you are cool. "Provide value first," Vaynerchuk says. "It gives you such a better chance."

If you're not sure where to begin with Twitter, seek out the people you admire most—thought leaders, keynote speakers, authors, colleagues—anyone who inspires you. You'll get a good sense of their topics of conversation and what their followers are most engaged in. It's also a good idea to follow your customers and even your competitors to see what they're up to.

Then, start retweeting useful or interesting information. You should also seek to provide interesting information that relates to your product or industry, or your community. "Your dialogue has to provide value. You're a local ice cream shop? Use your Twitter account to highlight good things local charities are doing or even a local Boy Scout troop.

If you're tweeting as yourself—as opposed to your company—don't be afraid to get personal, within certain limits. You don't want to broadcast everything about your day or your life, but occasionally tweeting the funny thing your teenager or your dog did can be a great way to humanize your company and connect with people.

For just about every product, industry, or topic, there are influential Twitter users. Connecting with them can make a big difference, either because they have a large number of followers (or highly influential followers), represent your biggest customers (such as a retail chain that might carry your product), or write an influential blog. Choose a dozen, and then build up to a hundred or two hundred. Follow them, and engage with them. You may be surprised by how many are willing to follow you back.

Think Real Time

During major global events, Twitter's usage rate can spike by millions of people across the world as they flock to the network. Users follow event specific hashtags and get insights from their favorite participants on the ground as they are happening and at the same time as the press. When you use a hashtag that's trending, you have a substantially better chance of getting engagement from people who aren't your followers, says Vaynerchuk. As the hashtag grows, you may get traction you wouldn't have otherwise. One way to take advantage of the new eyeballs is to pose your tweet in the form of a question that people will want to answer.

Beyond breaking news, Twitter's events calendar helps marketers stay aware of and potentially leverage significant global events that are relevant in some way to their brand. The calendar enables users to filter their search by location, type of event, and date, giving marketers the ability to plan out their strategy months in advance.

The event insights give users critical data from past events such as audience size, demographics, and more. Relevant hashtags are provided so that marketers can categorize their brand's tweets with the others related to the event; that way they appear in the most popular searches done by interested parties.

How Measurable Is It?

You can measure just about anything on Twitter. While viewing your tweet gives you some basic stats (like the number of comments, retweets, and likes), you might want to dig a bit deeper to find more valuable metrics. The Tweet Activity view lets you do just that: Just click on the bar graph icon and you'll be presented with a ton of information.

You can see data showing the number of impressions and total engagements, as well as a breakdown of the various engagements. Through that, you'll glean important details about how your tweet performed—and make decisions designed to increase future engagement. Here are a few metrics to keep an eye on:

→ **Impressions.** Impressions are the number of times people view your tweet. When this number is high, it seems that the other metrics follow the trend upward. Using strategic hashtags that are relevant to your content will help distribute your tweet to a wider audience beyond your followers, which will boost your impressions.

→ **Retweets.** Measuring retweets shows whether or not your tweets are being shared by your audience. When someone retweets, it exposes your tweet to their followers. Retweeting is one of the primary ways content goes viral on Twitter. To boost your own retweets, consider retweeting your followers more often. They will take notice and begin to reciprocate by retweeting you more often as well. Also, make sure to send over a quick thank you tweet to those who retweet you.

→ **Link Clicks.** Driving traffic to your website, blog posts, or videos should be the focus of your marketing efforts on Twitter. The end goal for a marketer on Twitter is always to successfully convince someone to leave the platform and go to your website where they can make a purchase of your product, buy your book, or hire you. Measuring the number of link clicks your tweets are generating is essential in determining your effectiveness on Twitter.

→ **Engagement Rate.** Your engagement rate shows the number of engagements divided by impressions. Depending on your industry, tweets with images or video may show a higher engagement rate.

→ **Profile Visits.** Twitter shows you how many people are visiting your profile—an indication that people want to learn more about you. Make sure your profile is complete and compelling when they get there. To generate more profile visits, be interesting! Give away some free information that compels people to want to know more about you. If your tweets are boring, nobody will visit your profile.

Not for Everyone

While Twitter might be a darling of the tech industry and valuable when it comes to staying up-to-date with what's happening in the world, for many businesses, it's not the best place to acquire new customers. "As a startup you have to pick a couple things and do it really well," says Corbett Drummey, CEO of Popular Pays, a company helping brands like Macy's, TOMS, and KIND connect with social influencers and content creators to execute Instagram, Snapchat, Pinterest, and Facebook campaigns. "If you were a makeup company you might do YouTube tutorials and Instagram. Or, if you are a lifestyle company you might just do Instagram and Facebook ads."

Twitter Tips Make TheBeautyBean.com

"I REALLY DON'T THINK I would have an online magazine if it weren't for Twitter," says Alexis Wolfer, founder of TheBeauty-Bean.com, an online beauty and health magazine for women. "I was working in an editorial job part-time and finishing graduate school and I wrote my thesis on women's magazines and their influence on body image," she explains. "And I started posting health, beauty, and nutrition tips on Twitter. They were much like what women's magazines would provide, except I took out all the focus on weight loss. It was all about healthy living, and in one month I had 1,000 followers."

Wolfer had already thought about starting an online magazine offering health and beauty tips without weight-loss advice. "Had I not received the Twitter response that I did, it would have been much slower to develop. But the response I got from Twitter in particular made me feel there were other women out there looking for healthy living information."

—

How Much Does It Cost?

Posting from your account is free. When it comes to advertising, Twitter is different than Facebook, LinkedIn, and Pinterest. Each of these social networks offer separate business/brand accounts and personal accounts. Advertising is only available to business accounts.

On Twitter, there are just accounts. Anytime you hit a little jackpot on Twitter and see something really taking off (whether it's a tweet you're pleased with or piece of content you want to promote) you don't need to set up a business page. You can just spend $50 against that post to amplify it.

When to Promote Your Tweets

Promoting your tweet allows you to increase the number of impressions, getting your message in front of the eyes of more users. If you press the Promote Your Tweet button, you'll be presented with a panel where you can select a target location, choose a spending budget, and plan an estimated reach if you decide to go forward.

Like other platforms, pricing is determined by supply and demand. There's no minimum cost. The more you pay, the more people in your desired audience will see the tweets appear in their feeds. In many cases, you can spend just a few dollars a day to do some testing and see what's resonating to help you decide where to put the most investment.

While you don't need to promote every tweet—and probably shouldn't—investing in the right ones can really pay off.

And, if you select your top-performing posts, the true unicorns in the bunch, the cost per click can actually be very low. Twitter uses an algorithm to determine the price, and engaging content is rewarded with lower costs.

To find your top-performing tweets (and confirm your suspicion that the epic meme you shared a while back really was solid gold), head over to the Analytics section. Then, select the Tweets tab and click the Top Tweets button.

Event activation enables you to link tweets to an upcoming event, like the Oscars or the Super Bowl. You can create paid campaigns targeting the event, then home in on the target audience by segmenting via gender, language, and even by the type of device they use.

Even more powerful is the ability to easily find and target the events that are most relevant to your company. Getting started is as easy as logging into ads.twitter.com and selecting Events Calendar from the Tools menu.

Can I DIY?

Yes. Just know that the deeper you delve into paid advertising, the more complex the calculus becomes. If you plan to run continual paid campaigns, a marketing expert can help make sure you're taking advantage of the ever-evolving suite of targeting tools and analytics, as well as help you iterate and evolve as your results come in.

INSTAGRAM

Instagram, the popular photo- and video-sharing app, counts 700 million monthly active users—and growing. Instagram users practically expect to interact with brands on the channel: More than 80 percent of those users follow a business on the app, making it an ideal platform for small business owners to reach potential customers.

Instagram is good for more than just posting selfies, brunches, and fur babies, as cute as they may be. And while it's known for being heavy on millennial and Gen Z women, they're not the only ones using the platform. At a time when visual content is critical for any brand to execute on a successful marketing strategy, Instagram presents a unique opportunity to position your brand creatively and showcase its personality. Plus, it's a place where your consumers can see your curated content every single day without feeling overwhelmed by emails and notifications. In fact, half of the platform's users check their feed multiple times a day.

Many small business owners say they simply don't know how to use Instagram. Don't be intimidated. Instagram is easy to use.

Start by creating the right kind of account. After you create a basic Instagram profile (or if you have one already), you'll want to upgrade it to an Instagram for Business account. This will give you access to features that personal users don't have. With an Instagram for Business account you can access more in-depth analytics and promote your posts, among other benefits.

When it comes to content, you probably want to keep the personal photos you share with family and friends separate from the business posts you share with customers. You can manage up to five Instagram accounts from one app, making it easy to switch between business and personal accounts, or multiple business accounts if you have several locations or product lines.

 ## Can I DIY?

You'll probably want to, at least as first. Managing your own Instagram—just like with Twitter—will help you come across as unfiltered and authentic. But don't just start throwing things on your page. Take the time to craft a strategy.

Your strategy starts with a goal. What do you want to do on Instagram? What are you hoping to get out of it?

You might decide that you want to use Instagram as a great way to build brand-name awareness. Or you might be thinking that Instagram is a great way to share pictures of your products because it's image focused.

Maybe you're just looking to land some direct sales from the link on your profile page. Whatever your goal, make sure you approach Instagram marketing with an eye toward fulfilling it. Then start looking for ways to gather your audience. Take it from John Lincoln, co-founder and CEO of digital marketing company Ignite Visibility. In fifty weeks, he says, he went from zero to more than 14,000 followers, and today, he gets about fifteen to thirty leads a month from Instagram for digital marketing services. His strategy involved a laser focus on an audience, followed by a concerted, consistent, and diligent publishing pattern.

Your audience might fall into one of two demographics: partners or customers. Partners are people in the same industry or in an industry related to your niche. They're not necessarily competitors, though. For example, if you're a web developer, then people who design WordPress themes might be among your partners. They complement, rather than compete, with your business. They can also help you promote your business.

How? By commenting on and liking your updates. They help give your Instagram account the appearance of authority. Then, there are Instagram followers who are in your target market. Those are the people whom you want to become customers.

Once you've identified partners and people in your target market, it's time to start gathering information about them, Lincoln says. What are their typical qualities? Where do they spend their time online? And, importantly: Who do they follow on Instagram?

Once you know that, you can inspire your target to follow you by imitating other accounts that they already follow.

Find between two and five Instagram accounts that your distributors and potential customers follow, Lincoln suggests, and analyze them. What kind of content do they post online? Who follows them? Also take a look at their bio. How do they describe their business? What does the profile photo look like?

Go through their posts and look at the hashtags they use. Make a note of the most popular hashtags. You'll probably want to use those in your own posts. It's important, though, to make sure that the post corresponds to the hashtag you use. Otherwise, you'll be branded a spammer.

Finally, take a look at their most popular posts. Make a note about the types of photos used in those posts and the topics they cover.

Start a Conversation

Yes, Instagram is primarily a visual platform, but you can also use copy to connect with customers. When you share a post, include a question in the photo caption and prompt your customers to respond in the comments section. When they post a comment, make sure you reply. Make it a conversation.

Create unique posts and engage users in a personal way that affects people on an emotional level. Know why you're posting what you're posting. And don't forget to participate in the conversation! It's invaluable to show your followers that you care.

You might be thinking, Okay, so I'm doing all of that. Those are the basics. If you still don't feel like you're getting the traction you want, here are a few tips:

- **Show your personality.** Define your point of view and be consistent. Are you funny? Inspirational? Heartfelt? Sarcastic? What are you trying to say and to whom are you trying to say it?

- **Engage your users.** Sure, Instagram is a bit self-involved, so use that to your advantage. Users love to see themselves re-grammed by brands that they love. Reusing content is also free. Run contests and giveaways to source user generated content (UGC) and build your audience.

- **Show your fans who you are behind the scenes.** Be authentic and do away with the veneer.

- **Use hashtags** both to increase impressions and to generate UGC. Want inspiration in that vein? Search #Starbucks and you'll see an example.

- **Promote your ads.** Yes, you need to put money where your posts are if you want to see results.

- **Know your goals**, engagement versus conversion, and how to optimize posts for each. How do you know? A/B testing is the only way to really know for sure, since the mix up is different for every brand.

Don't Try to Be Perfect

Much has been made of the move toward perfectly curated imagery on Instagram. Food is styled like a magazine cover, products are shot in perfect light, outfits are labored over. (The same holds true for other social channels, too, but Instagram has been held up as the prime example of the trend.)

While that kind of high-intensity styling stood out in Instagram's early days, today it's starting to feel a bit tired—and a bit inauthentic, which is anathema to the intended mission of social channels. Plus, everyone's feeds start to look alike: No one stands out when everyone is producing the same hyper-polished imagery. So rather than trying to keep up with the beauty arms race, bow out.

You don't need flawless, perfectly lit shots of your products, your store, or your people. To recapture attention, you need to go back to basics. Channel the less-curated, more spontaneous vibe of Instagram's early days. Make a play for genuineness. Better yet, let people into your imperfection, with candid shots and notes on what goes on when no one is watching. It may help you stand out—and connect—more than hiring a specialized photographer ever will.

Use the Right Hashtags

Hashtags—words or phrases preceded by the "#" symbol—are everywhere. Using the right hashtags will help new followers find your business. For instance, if a potential customer taps the #OutdoorKitchen hashtag on another landscape designer's post, they would see a list of all posts with that hashtag, including yours.

Small business owners should use common hashtags related to their business:

> Your industry or field, like #Plumbing, #Remodeling or #LandscapeDesign

> Your products, like #Cabinets, #SwimmingPools or #Furniture

> Special features or qualities, like #MadeInAmerica, #Handmade or #ShopLocal

While you can create any hashtag you want, it won't do any good if others don't know to use or search for your hashtag. So, if you create a unique hashtag for your business, make sure you promote it on your website, email newsletters, or with in-store displays.

Great content, says Vaynerchuk, can be incredibly effective when it's amplified with hashtags. Hashtags create discoverability and organic amplification for your content.

Add Your Location

When you share a photo or video on Instagram, you can tag the image with the location where it was taken. Posts tagged with your company location will display your name and address just above the image. Instagram users can then tap on your location name and see:

→ Your location on a map

→ Other photos and videos you've tagged along with your business information

→ Photos and videos your customers have tagged along with your business information

It's easy to add a location to your posts. Look for the "Add Location" option when you're getting ready to share a new photo or video. A list of suggested locations will appear beneath this prompt; if your business is listed, tap to add it to your image. If your company doesn't automatically show up, tap "Search" or "Add Location" for a longer list of suggested locations.

Create an Editorial Calendar

If you want to move ahead of your competition on social media, you may want to create an editorial calendar. A schedule of your upcoming posts, telling you what you'll post and when you'll post it, will keep you honest and make sure your posting frequency stays as you intend it.

A calendar, though, can be intimidating when you see all those posting dates stretching out in front of you. If you're struggling to maintain volume and come up with new ideas, when you're planning your content, copy the type of content that others have used successfully and use it yourself. If they're posting popular new products or photos from events, try the same approach. Imitation isn't just the sincerest form of flattery. It's also a great way to promote your brand.

Clearly that doesn't mean running afoul of copyright laws, so don't take anything verbatim or lift images. You can, however, post content that's related to the successful posts of others. There's nothing wrong with that.

Once you've got your editorial calendar in place, it's time to start following it—but don't post and disappear. Engage with other Instagram users. Follow accounts in your niche and accounts related to your niche. Like and comment on posts you appreciate.

If you're viewed as an active member of the Instagram community, you'll come across as a genuine user and not somebody who's just trying to sell something. Plus, you'll often get a follow back from the people you follow. That's especially true if they're interested in your business.

Another thing to do: Look at the top profiles in your niche. Then, go through some of their posts. Follow people who are commenting on those posts. These are the most engaged people, so there is a chance they will engage with you also.

All of this will help your posts show up in Instagram search, which can send more people to your profile and business.

Tell Your Story

Instagram Stories is a feature that allows users to create slideshows using photos, video, text, and graphics. Stories are displayed at the very top of a user's feed—a prominent place to get your followers' attention.

Each Story disappears after twenty-four hours, making it a good showcase for visual content that's both immediate and temporary, such as:

→ Behind-the-scenes tours of your business

→ Introductions of new team members

→ Demos of new products or services

→ Timely news, such as a grand opening, sale, or event

To create a Story, tap the "Your Story" button at the top left of your Instagram home screen. From here you can record a video, or if you swipe down you can select from photos you've taken recently. You can add text, draw on top of your photos or videos with the paint tool, or add fun graphical stickers.

One big advantage of Stories: Unlike with regular posts, you can see how many people view your story along with their names, so you'll know exactly which customers you're reaching on Instagram.

Huckberry Masters Composition and Color

A FEW COMPANIES HAVE figured out how to quickly amass huge Instagram followings—and turn followers into customers.

Men's outdoor gear company Huckberry is one. The San Francisco company launched its Instagram campaign in earnest in September 2014. By January 2016, it had 154,000 followers and counting, wooing them with a combination of beautiful photography and careful strategy.

While the return on investment is tough to track, Huckberry's managing editor at the time, Zach Pina, estimated that one like this could bring in $10,000 in sales—in this case, much of it from Huckberry's stock of fall watches, leather boots, and heavy-duty "duck canvas" shirts and pants.

Composition and color are essential to create posts that stand out as users scroll through their feeds. Your selfie game might be strong, but leave the photo-taking to a professional if you can. This doesn't mean you need to break the bank. While Huckberry has paid photographers, it generally gets its Instagram art from partners (Huckberry sells other clothing companies' products, for example) or employees with photography backgrounds. The most important thing: Be sure the subject matter is in line with what your followers expect from your brand.

Create a posting calendar, and exercise restraint—you don't want to oversaturate your audience. An occasional strategy: Try drumming up interest for a sale with a preview post. Huckberry once teased a sale on vintage Rolex watches with an ambiguous macro shot, and then followed it up thirty-six hours later with the big reveal. The watches moved quickly—$85,000 in sales in one week.

Huckberry's playful language appeals to the whiskey lovers in its outdoorsy demographic. Captions that are relatable, funny, or highly informative—even about something other than your products—make users that much more likely to like your posts (some of Huckberry's rack up more than 6,000 such endorsements) or to tag their friends. Pina writes the posts himself: "People want to see who you really are," he says. "Find your voice, hone it, and then stay super consistent."

—

LaCroix Features Followers

THOUGH LACROIX IS NOT the only fizzy water on the market, it's emerging as the brand of choice. Sales more than doubled from 2014 to 2016, to $225.5 million, *The Wall Street Journal* reported.[3] A key part of its marketing plan: a rock-solid Instagram strategy that's targeted toward millennials.

You probably haven't seen LaCroix commercials on TV. Instead, you'll find them across social media. "We strived for 100 percent consumer involvement by acknowledging all comments about LaCroix and responding to our fans on a daily basis," writes former digital LaCroix strategist Alma Pantaloukas on LinkedIn.

The company encourages its followers to use branded hashtags like #LaCroixlove and #LiveLaCroix for a chance to be featured on their profile. And, they use trending hashtags to align their brand with what's hot. An example: LaCroix is reposting user photos with the hashtag #Whole30approved. Whole30 is a month-long "eating healthy" program that eschews processed foods, sugar, dairy, and grains. As you can imagine, a lot of foods aren't permitted on the program. But LaCroix is.

These tactics not only attract new users to their social-media circle, but also show LaCroix as a social-media savvy brand that "gets" its target audience.

How Much Does It Cost?

Just posting on Instagram is free. If you're reliant on professional photography, you may pay a few hundred dollars for each shoot—but you can also try to find a student or part-time photographer to keep costs down.

If you elect to promote posts, you can promote a single image, a carousel of images, or a video. Plus, an ad allows you the opportunity to add a link. You decide how long the ad will run and set the budget—Instagram advertising works much the same way as its corporate parent, Facebook. As of 2017, the average cost per click was heading toward the $1 mark, according to one study from AdEspresso.[4]

How Measurable Is It?

Very. After a few months of Instagram marketing, take some time to review what's working best for you.

Go over your analytics. Make a note of the types of posts that receive the most engagement. Be sure to publish posts with similar themes in the future. Make a note of what types of posts are receiving the least engagement. Scratch those kinds of posts off your editorial calendar if there any more like them coming up. Replace them with the kinds of posts that are more successful.

PINTEREST

Pinterest, more than any other social network, is about buying stuff. A 2015 Millward Brown study found that 93 percent of users who were active in the previous six months used the site to plan purchases.[5] You read that right: 93 percent.

Pinterest users deliberately integrate brand relationships into life planning and major milestones: The Millward Brown study found that active Pinners were 47 percent more likely to experience a major life event in the next six months—and, more tellingly, were disproportionately using Pinterest to plan for their events. If your audience is on Pinterest—and that's a big if—it's a natural place to engage meaningfully with consumers and is a great way to quickly boost traffic to your website.

This network may be the most underused, especially considering it has 150 million active monthly users and boasts what Popular Pays' Corbett Drummey calls "amazing shopability."[6] It's the ideal medium for any company that wants to sell fashion, home products, or other things to women sitting at their computers. "You can either use promoted pins or work with people who really know the medium."

Research Your Audience

You may think of Pinterest as a site for recipes, weddings, and DIY home decorating. For that reason, you may be reluctant to use it—or, you may pigeonhole the content you choose to share there. It's true that Pinterest is about those things—but not only those things.

As with other social strategies, it's important to first know who your audience is and where they are. If you know that your target audience hangs out on Pinterest, then you are in a prime position to learn more about them—even if they're there to plan their wedding, and you make financial-planning software. Use Pinterest to see what your target audience is interested in: What problems do they have? What content do they engage with the most? Use that knowledge to your advantage as you create your products and services, and when you market them. Get a feel for how your competitors are using their pages, too.

As with other social platforms, don't be disingenuous. If you're a financial services company, you better have a compelling reason to be pinning about interior decorating. Potential customers will see right through you. But if you can connect with your audience authentically in a moment that's important to them—for example, financial planning when you're getting married or buying a home—you maintain your credibility.

Refine Your Profile

Once you know who on Pinterest you want to attract, take some time to update your profile. Update your profile name, description, and profile image to make sure it's immediately clear who you are and how you help people. Create clearly named and logically organized dedicated boards that are relevant to the themes, questions, challenges, and interests of the audience you want to be attracting, and fill them with relevant pins.

If you're already active on Pinterest, this may mean you need to remove some of your existing boards and pins that are not relevant to your defined target audience's interest. (If you want to save those pins for your own reference later, switch the boards to private so that only you will be able to see them, and they won't dilute the focus of your profile and brand.)

Set Up Your Pinterest Business Page

It's important to make sure that you create a business page as opposed to a personal page because it gives you access to more features, such as analytics and rich pins.

Most companies start out by creating a board and then uploading pins to that board.

To create a board, you simply click *Create a Board* that will show up on your profile page, fill out the name of your board, description, category, if you want to include a map, if you want it to be a secret board (a board only you and those you invite can see), and any collaborators you want to add to the board. You may potentially want to add collaborators to make sure that someone in every department has access should they want to include something on Pinterest for your business. Click *Create* and you're set.

Once you're on your homepage, you want to visit your profile page to see everything that your company has added. Click the Pin icon in the upper-right-hand corner. You will see all of your boards, and if you click each board, you will see your pins, or all the individual content you posted.

Create Pins

Once you're set up, it's time to start creating pins—the content people are going to see, repin to their own boards, and use to buy or share. In other words, your pins are crucial.

To create a pin, visit the board you want to pin to and click *Add a Pin*. You then have the option to add a pin from the web or from your computer. In order to really stand out and hopefully earn some shares on the network, funny gifs and memes from the web are a great option, but the best option is to upload your own content. Regardless of which option you pick, web or upload, you'll be able to write a description and then publish.

Pinterest is really just a giant, visual search engine. Like on Google, when a user searches Pinterest for a particular term or string of words, they're shown content that's deemed the most relevant and high-quality results related to that search term. The goal is to have your pins show up in the top posts for the keywords that your audience is searching for.

Defining your target audience likely helped surface some key terms and phrases that your audience is interested in, but Pinterest makes it easy to know what's most relevant. When you type a general keyword into Pinterest's search area, and hit *enter*, Pinterest will show and suggest popular keywords related to the original term you put in. This will give you great ideas for search terms to optimize for.

Once you have a list of keywords, start adding them to the description area of your pins and your boards. If it's possible and natural, try to weave them into your profile name and description, too.

Keep in mind, whatever you want to upload to Pinterest must include an image or a video in order to be accepted and added by the network. Rules aside, Pinterest is a visual medium with a sophisticated visual search engine: Every pin should be as visually compelling as possible. This doesn't mean sticking to product photography, though: Pinners love infographics, step-by-step tutorials ("instructographics"), and before-and-afters. Convey your brand philosophy and messages in high-quality images and use text sparingly. Pay attention to trending images and categories, and learn by example.

Pinterest is all about aspiration or utility, notes Gary Vaynerchuk. If you're selling wine, teach people about how to read a label, what's significant about a new wine you just received, or the difference between varietals. "People are shopping on Pinterest, so they're spending more time on the content and looking at it with a critical eye," he says.

Do Some Quick Repinning

A "repin" means that you pin content other users have added onto your boards. Like on Twitter and Facebook, browsing and repinning others' content is important for visibility. This helps you get noticed by others on Pinterest and hopefully jumpstart your own pins.

To find content you may want to repin to your boards, you can search keywords in the search bar, look through categories that are similar, or just scroll through your homefeed. Hover over the image, click *Pin It*, choose the board you want the pin to go to, and you're done.

Rich pins allow you to add extra information to all of your pins. By adding rich pins, you can help give visitors more information about your brand, which can help you stand out more among your competition. There are five different types of rich pins, including recipe and movie pins, but below are the three most often used for small businesses (and particularly B2B businesses):

→ **Place pins.** This means that those who pin something you have enabled with place pins will be able to put it on their map.

→ **Article pins.** This is a pin that has an image along with an article link.

→ **Product pins.** This shows users where they can purchase the pin they're looking at, the price, and the website link to make the purchase. Users can even buy directly through Pinterest.

Schedule and Loop Your Pins

Pinterest's algorithm strongly weighs how often you pin quality content, and prioritizes accounts that are adding it every day. While this might seem overwhelming, there are ways to make it less of a burden on your calendar.

Certain tools allow you to loop your pins, or repin the content you've already pinned to help create a steady stream of activity. The result is that your account always looks active and engaged.

But using a scheduler isn't an excuse to neglect "live" pinning, since Pinterest also likes recent and new content, too. A few minutes each day will pay off. Pinterest's algorithm also weighs engagement pretty heavily when it's ranking content, seeing comments, likes, and repins as a sign that content is high quality. This means it's important for you to engage with (and earn engagement from) other pinners in order to drive up your placement in search results.

Make Sure You're Traffic Ready

But optimizing your Pinterest presence is really just the first step. Once users click a pin and head to your website, you need to have optimized the path you want them to take, such as signing up for your email list or joining a course.

You're in trouble if you spent all of your time on pins leading to your website, but your site isn't ready for the traffic. Wherever a pinner lands on your site, it should be clear what the site is and what the user will get out of it. That's critically important since you're likely connecting with a new audience.

If you're using Pinterest to grow your email list, be sure to add opt-in registration forms on your website in multiple places so that new visitors will be invited to join. As a bonus, you can offer an incentive for users to join the list. For digital product or service-based businesses, that could be checklists, worksheets, or guidebooks. For software as a service (SaaS) businesses, free trials are a great option.

You also want to build a mailing list of people who love what you do. While this may not be a way to directly earn income, it is definitely a piece of the puzzle. Use Pinterest as a path to get people to sign up for your mailing list.

If you have a service-based business, Pinterest is a great way for you to connect with your potential clients. Use it to share testimonials, your portfolio, motivational quotes, and even tips and tools that they can use. Show them what they stand to gain by working with you.

 ## How Measurable Is It?

Pinterest has a robust built-in analytics platform. It includes the usual suspects:

- → Average daily impressions
- → Average daily viewers
- → Audience location
- → Gender and language of audience
- → Number of repins
- → Amount of clicks
- → Total likes

You can also see which pins are driving traffic to your website.

 ## How Much Does It Cost?

Setting up a profile and pinning is free. Ads on Pinterest are called Promoted Pins—they are like regular pins, but you're paying so that they appear in more of your desired audiences' feeds. Like other social media channels, you pay per 1,000 impressions—there's no minimum fee. You simply choose the already-created pin you want to promote and specify a budget and a maximum bid.

Pinterest's built-in analytics will show you all the standard fare, such as impressions, engagement, and clicks. You can also pay a third-party vendor for deeper analysis of just about any metric, like conversion to in-store sales. You may pay a subscription or a percentage of conversions.

Find Affiliates

Many companies and small business owners offer their customers the opportunity to become an affiliate. An affiliate is someone who uses a product or service and then promotes that product in exchange for a portion of the profit when someone decides to place an order through their link.

Pinterest banned affiliate links in 2015 and then reopened the platform to them in 2016. Today, you can use popular images and your customized affiliate link to catch people's attention, tell them about the product, and send them to where they need to go to place an order.

A good affiliate marketing program should have leveraged income. When people you sign up have others sign up, you can make money from those sales as well.

Affiliate marketing on Pinterest can be a low-cost way to widen your audience. You only pay if the affiliate generates a sale for you. The commission could be anywhere from single digits to 30 percent or more, depending on your industry and the size of a typical sale.

SNAPCHAT

Let's just clear the air: You may think of Snapchat as the "sexting" app. That's the reputation Snapchat started with, though the company has worked hard to shed it. Known for so-called "ephemeral" messaging (because its main feature is quickly disappearing messages, known as *snaps*), Snapchat has the youngest audience of any major messaging app.

If your goal is to connect with a younger audience, Snapchat may be a great place to do that. Its stigma shed, you can now find companies as large as airlines and as small as solo entrepreneurs building their image and engaging with followers. The content they're sharing through stories and videos is unlike anything you can find on other platforms, which is why many businesses are hesitant to jump into these less-tested waters.

Snapchat works like other social media channels. You can follow people and they can follow you back. There's a twist, though. When people take pictures or videos and send them to their friends on Snapchat, those images don't hang around in a timeline forever like they do on Instagram. Instead, they're deleted after at most ten seconds (the exact amount of time is determined by the sender). Users can also send *stories*. Those are collections of snaps and videos that are broadcast to all followers instead of individual users—a usage more relevant to most businesses than individual snaps.

During the fourth quarter of 2016, Snapchat reached 70 percent of eighteen- to twenty-four-year-olds, according to analysis from MoffettNathanson.[7] While older users are tiptoeing in, the channel still skews very young. Those who do use it, however, tend to spend a lot of time there, making it ripe ground for brands that target younger markets and want to get in early.

How to Use It

Snapchat's point of differentiation is its urgency. If content is going to disappear, users are more likely to engage with it now, before it's gone forever. Users are more likely to click on a twenty-four-hour Snapshot Story if they'll be unable to view that same content the following day. The fear of missing something important can be potent.

Because snaps are understood to be of-the-moment, unpolished, and personal, there's a genuine and authentic element associated with them—they're intended to be unvarnished, conversational, spontaneous. This is why Snapchat users tend to use the platform to engage with close ties and romantic interests more than with the distant acquaintances they may engage with via Facebook.

Some things you can do:

→ Take users behind the scenes

→ Offer exclusive videos and image content

→ Run contests

→ Preview new products

→ Offer tips or hacks for using your products

→ Announce promotions or sales

If you're not regularly posting content, then people have no reason to follow you. They're not going to talk about you, or engage with you, when you never show up in their "recent" section.

You don't necessarily need a posting calendar for Snapchat, but you should be posting something daily so you have fresh content every twenty-four hours (since old snaps are done at the twenty-four-hour mark and are removed). This way your brand is always in followers' recent updates section.

Whenever you snap, save the content and be sure to share it in other places with a call to action to follow you for fun, entertainment, news, promotions, exclusive discounts, giveaways, etc., so you're leveraging those who aren't on the platform and drawing attention to it.

Snapchat's closest social media cousin is Instagram: Both feature timed videos and visual content. At the moment, the main points of differentiation are audience and reach: For now, Instagram Stories has a significantly wider reach and receives more engagement, but Snapchat continues to dominate among younger users. Snapchat is a natural place to deliver calls to action; because Snapchat content disappears quickly, those CTAs come with built in urgency.

Like Instagram, Snapchat offers lenses and filters that allow a user to manipulate an image—those are some of the platform's most-used features. As more platforms continue to offer overlapping features, brands and marketers will have to be increasingly selective about which ones they invest in. Take advantage of analytics and reporting features to identify which platforms could offer you the best return.

 ### Can I DIY?

Definitely. Users on the platform expect content that's less polished and doesn't feel like a commercial. If you choose to go it alone, however, know that the platform is constantly evolving. You'll need to be diligent to keep up with new features and capabilities.

How Much Does It Cost?

Snapchat has been adding new paid features in an effort to attract more advertisers, including video ads and sponsored geofilters and lenses. Three of Snapchat's most popular paid marketing options are sponsored lenses, geofilters, and Snap Ad videos.

Snapchat has upped its game for small businesses—perhaps following a page from Facebook's playbook. For example, Snapchat has introduced a self-serve ad buying platform as well as a new creative tool called Snapchat Publisher, which lets advertisers of all sizes create full screen video ads in less than two minutes. So once Snapchat gets new advertisers on board to try advertising on it through incentives, it can then easily point them in the direction of the self-serve and creative publisher tools.

For some local businesses, geofilters—sort of like a photobooth skin—may be appealing. Because they cover just a small local area, they can cost as little as a few dollars, with the price increasing based on how much territory you include and how long you make the geofilter available. A few dollars can quickly become a few thousand if the ad is expanded to include a whole city or beyond.

How Measurable Is It?

It's hard—but getting easier. Users of Snapchat have always been able to track the standard stable of vanity metrics: open rates, story completions, and screenshots, which measure how often users save a snap. Recently, Snapchat has added third-party data collection to track ROI or paid campaigns. The company also recently added the ability to add in-app URLs—a long-awaited change for marketers and one that brings the app's capabilities closer to Instagram.

Finding B2B Success

BUSINESS COACH JON WESTENBERG has been pursuing what he calls "Snapchat experiments," playing with the way it encourages individual, one-on-one connection and engagement. The results, he says, have been "incredible."

Westenberg launched a new Snapchat show, called Lightbulb Moments, where he posts short videos and snaps that provide some simple business advice for his audience—businesses looking for business coaching and marketing advice. Every time, he asks people to post a snap back with just a lightbulb emoji. When they do, Westenberg offers one piece of advice tailored to their business.

After that interaction, Westenberg offers some information on his entry-level coaching and consulting programs—plus a link to get started.

"That level of deep one-on-one interaction has already been paying off," Westenberg says. He earned $3,000 in the first twenty-four hours of the initiative, and it's been steadily growing from there—a direct result, he says, of the personal engagement the channel offers.

To promote the new channel, he makes sure to list his Snapcode in his email signature, on his website, and on his Twitter. He also continually posts Snapchat stories, with tips for business owners, "to train our audience to expect great content."

Says Westenberg, "We engage, we talk, and we focus on individual followers. That last part is pretty crucial."

Who's Doing It Well

Aer Lingus was among the first airlines to make the move to Snapchat, using it as a promotional channel. It shares live content from events like inaugural flights, takes followers into cockpits, and creates stories with clear narratives.

Audi earned widespread accolades for one of the first successful Snapchat campaigns after teaming up with *The Onion* during Super Bowl XLVIII. Its sharing of banal stock images with unexpected, witty captions was simple but generated 100,000 views and 37 million social impressions, according to Audi's social media agency, Huge.

It's natural to think of something like Snapchat for consumer-facing products, but some B2B shops are finding a niche there as well. IBM uses Snapchat to offer an inside look at the new technologies they are developing. "On Snapchat, it's critical right from the start to establish why people should continue watching your story," says Katie Keating, global social brand strategy lead at IBM.[8] Keating suggests treating Snapchat's stories like any traditional story, featuring a start, beginning, and an ending. "It's easy once you start snapping to take for granted that you are immersed in the experience, but the Snapchat audience is not. Make sure to paint a robust picture to keep them interested," she advises.

YOUTUBE

YouTube is the second largest search engine in the world—and its owner happens to be Google, the largest search engine in the world.

But it is incredibly crowded. It would take 65 years to watch the new content uploaded to YouTube each day.[9]

All of that makes creating stand-out YouTube content a challenge. But that doesn't mean there isn't room for the channel as part of your marketing mix. You just have to know how to use it to your favor.

If you're already creating video content—whether it's how-to videos, tutorials, or something else—consider hosting that content on YouTube, even if you want the videos to run on your own site. Since Google acquired YouTube, videos hosted on the site get credence in search results. Plus, YouTube is mobile friendly, which is increasingly important as more and more consumers watch video from their phones.

What Kind of Video Is Right for Me?

If you're starting from scratch, your goal is to use YouTube content to build a loyal audience, one that consistently watches your videos and interacts with you.

First, just like other social channels, create content for your users—content that considers your audiences' needs first. That means your goal is not gimmicky content. While the number of views a video receives is certainly a valuable metric, it's not the most valuable one. You ultimately want people to view your videos and follow through with an actionable response. If you're producing videos just for views, you'll end up with very little of the latter.

Instead, focus on creating meaningful content by asking yourself the following questions before you start scripting: Is this video relevant to my audience? Will they find it exciting or informative? How will the average viewer respond after viewing the video?

Depending on the type of business, you may find success considering your customers' needs before and after their purchase. Before they buy, they're likely to watch product reviews. After they buy, they may look for fellow customers—just consider the success of "unboxing" videos, where buyers share the contents of new products they've bought, methodically taking all of the parts out of the box.

No matter what type of video you have, be consistent with the type of videos you're creating. Consumers thrive on familiarity and enjoy recurring characters and themes. You can do that in a number of ways: using the same presenter, or the same formula, or applying the same format to different subject matter (i.e., "top ten" videos). Creating videos around a consistent theme may help people become more comfortable with your brand.

Whatever you decide to produce, do it consistently. While many brands are good at creating quality videos, few are successful at *consistently* creating quality videos. Much like you do with your social media accounts and blogs, you need to invest in consistent content if you want to build an engaged community.

But I Want to Go Viral

First—trust us. You're not the first to decide that making a viral video would be great for your business. Over the last 15 years, thousands of marketing consultants and ad agencies have tried to crack the code of virality. It hasn't happened yet. That doesn't mean making one is impossible—but it's hardly as simple as adhering to a replicable formula.

If you want to give viral video a try, keep in mind that everyone's trying to do it. You'll miss the mark a lot more than you succeed. And while there's nothing wrong with taking a shot at the moon, even if you succeed, it's not sustainable. It's a great one-time way to increase exposure and acquire traffic, but it's not going to work long term.

Dollar Shave Club Masters Humor and Savvy Timing

MICHAEL DUBIN IS THE founder of Venice, California's Dollar Shave Club, which boasts millions of subscribers who pay as little as $1 a month, plus shipping, for a monthly delivery of razors. In 2016, the company was acquired by Unilever for a reported $1 billion. Dollar Shave Club got its first big boost from a 2012 YouTube video in which Dubin stars, that cost $4,500 and took a single day to shoot. It went supernova-viral in seventy-two hours. He told *Inc.* how it happened:

> I studied sketch and improv at the Upright Citizens Brigade training center in New York City for eight years. I know humor is a very powerful device in telling a story. I never thought twice about appearing in the video; I wasn't really going to hire someone else to do that. I didn't necessarily think that I was going to become the spokesman of the company in addition to the CEO. I was just really trying to find a fun, resonant way to tell the story of what our business did and why it existed. We chose YouTube as a platform to spread the word about DSC because [at that time] YouTube was the only place to go if you wanted any hope of going viral.

We also announced our $1 million seed round of funding the day the video launched. We purposely delayed our funding announcement to time it with the video launch and a relaunch of the website. All the usual suspects covered the three events: TechCrunch, etc. From there, the mainstream media picked up on them, and the video took off.

The events were designed to coincide with one another so we would get the maximum thrust on the video. We also timed it to go up just before South by Southwest. Everyone was talking about the video while they were in Austin, so strategically it ended up being a pretty smart move.

Unfortunately, our servers were totally unprepared for the amount of traffic that flooded in. Our first video went live at 6:00 a.m. PT on March 6, 2012. By 7:30 a.m., the site had crashed and we couldn't get it back up for 24 hours. I was terrified that, in that moment, my biggest dreams were turning into my worst nightmares.

The next day the site was back up, we had twelve thousand new subscribers, and within just a few days, three million people had watched the video. Since then, we've produced another; collectively both have been viewed more than 25 million times. It was a fantastic way to come out of the gate and raise awareness of our mission. I don't think you could have accomplished that any other way.

If you do decide it's viral or bust, keep the following must-have attributes in mind:

→ **Simple.** Viral video content must be short and simple. People have short attention spans and are likely to be viewing content on Facebook and Twitter. Users want to be able to click on something, quickly consume, share, and move on. Keep videos under two minutes—preferably shorter.

→ **Unique.** This goes without saying. No one's going to share something that has a been-there-done-that vibe.

→ **Timely.** Most viral videos are timely and relevant. This is usually the most difficult aspect for marketers, as it requires you to stay up to date on current topics and react quickly.

The strategy works well for tutorials and DIY videos aimed at niche audiences, or for any brand which wants to track conversions. It's often not the best strategy for mass market brands, some of which have learned the hard way that YouTube's comment section can be ruthless and unrelentingly critical. Instagram and Snapchat tend to offer kinder, gentler comments sections.

 Can I DIY?

Yes, but it can be tricky. Consumers these days expect polished looking video—even if it's shot on an iPhone and designed to look casual and off-the-cuff. You can hire a video producer for an hourly consulting rate. Or, if you want a true commercial-grade video, seek out a video partner who understands how to develop and scale branded video that shines in today's chaotic landscape. You may be charged anywhere from a couple thousand dollars to more than $15,000, depending on the scope of the project and the type of partner you select.

CONTENT MARKETING

Few marketing concepts in the last decade have generated as much buzz—and stronger opinions—than content marketing. The furor, which had been gaining steam already, really took off in 2008 when Seth Godin famously opined that content marketing "is all the marketing that's left."

But what does that mean, really—and what *is* content marketing, exactly?

The backbone of content marketing is engaging an audience consistently so its members are naturally attracted to your brand. The idea is that traditional "push" marketing—where you send an outbound message like an ad—is dead in an era of marketing saturation. Consumers—particularly younger ones—tune out overt marketing messages. Content marketing, which started as the idea of creating content that helps consumers, with the side benefit of generating interest and ultimately, selling, is the antithesis of the traditional "push."

One other note: We've put content marketing in the Online Marketing section of this book, because small businesses most commonly start their content initiatives with online articles, blogs or videos. But content marketing doesn't have to be online. Branded magazines were one of the original forms of content marketing, and they remain relevant today. Just look at mattress company Casper, which shuttered its online content site in 2017—and launched a glossy magazine instead.

What Should My Content Be About?

Knowing what your ideal customers want to better understand is the first step to knowing what to write about. Go back to those personas that we talked about in the beginning of this book. They incorporated not just demographic data about your customers, like age, gender, and location, but also psychographics—the "why" behind their buying decisions. They also considered specific needs your ideal customer might have when it comes to your business or product.

Each piece of content you create should be targeted to a specific persona, with a specific need. Once you know who you're talking to, you can map their questions and needs to the most appropriate step in your customer's journey. Are they looking for information on how to set up their company's servers? Do they need customer service tips? Or style advice? Mapping unmet needs to your customer's journey gives much needed context—and relevance—to the content you create.

Successful content marketing requires that you get out of your own head. Too many companies create content that they might think is important, but their customers don't need or want.

How Do I Execute?

First, decide who's making the content. You can either create original content or curate content. Some founders feel extremely comfortable penning their own content, while others outsource. The advantage to keeping the task in-house is twofold: It's cheap (just your time) and it really sounds like the company, because you *are* the company.

The downsides: It takes an incredible commitment to create an ongoing stream of content. More than you realize. And most people are not writers. It's hard to view your own writing objectively, and a professional can help you shape copy that not only tells the best story it can, but also is positioned in a way that your intended audience will find compelling.

That's why companies often look to hire writers to create their content marketing for them—someone to come in and make them look good. Hiring a writer can make a lot of sense, says Erik Sherman, an *Inc.* columnist and content marketer. A pro can help structure what you have, find better ways of saying it, and even bring together different insights. He notes that he's worked on projects where a small handful of people with a journalistic background went into a company and found important things that employees knew, which then turned into strong marketing pieces.

To make sure an outsider doesn't helicopter into your company and write something that sounds generic or not reflective of you, make sure the writer interviews you or your employees on specific subjects. They can get on the phone for an hour or so to talk to the expert. Often there is a specific topic at hand, but sometimes the discussion is more open ended—and someone with a journalistic background may ferret out a new story angle that you had never considered.

At that point, the writer can develop an outline, submit it for review, pull together the piece, and then have the expert (and people in marketing and possibly legal, of course) review the content. Or you could have someone on the inside write the piece and work with an editor to ensure it is readable. What you have at that point is content marketing that can demonstrate your competitive differentiation, insight, and topic knowledge. Whether it's written or heavily edited by someone outside your organization, it breathes your company.

Blue Apron Offers a Recipe for Community

MEAL KIT DELIVERY SERVICE Blue Apron uses content to generate excitement about a dish before it's ever delivered to the door. The company knows that its recipes may be a bit more exotic than its customers are accustomed to cooking. Leading up to the release of a recipe, the Blue Apron team creates fun articles about the dish, where it came from, what techniques are used, and any traditions surrounding it. "We want people to cook because it's fun, so we equip them with knowledge on our website—even if they don't use our service," says vice president of marketing Rani Yadav. "We find this to be the best way to build trust and loyalty."

When subscribers finally do cook a particular dish, they're knowledgeable about their creation and want to show it off. To date, Blue Apron has cultivated 1.8 million fans on Facebook, many of whom proudly showcase their masterpieces. "The engagement on social is what's most astounding," Rani says. "You can't buy people to comment and talk about your brand with the love and enthusiasm that our community does. And these are people who would never talk to each other in the real world, but on our social-media channels they're sharing tips about cooking bok choy—it's so fun to see!"

It's a common practice for websites to "sell" their visitors at every turn—but as this particular story illustrates, that's not often the best strategy when it comes to content. Blue Apron was able to identify a genuine need among their audience—cooking tips and information—and delivers that information in a non-salesy way that cultivates sharing and conversation.

"Everything we do is in service of making cooking fun and easy for our home chefs," she says. "By using that lens to develop content, product features, and recipes, we're able to create an experience that our customers want to make part of their daily lives, and they stick with us. We constantly get love letters from customers saying we've saved their marriage, given them confidence in the kitchen, or helped them get their kids interested in cooking. That customer feedback motivates our team every day."

—

Manage the Process

Similar to how you may handle certain social channels, the best way to streamline your content creation process is to create an editorial calendar. Plan out your calendar in advance with new content ideas on a regular basis, such as yearly or quarterly. Your exact process will depend on a variety of factors, including your team and the resources you have available. The cadence of your content production will depend on where you're publishing, what your audience needs, and the resources you have.

You can distribute content through your own blog, other blogs, email, social media—wherever you're connecting with your audience. This is where content marketing begins to overlap with social marketing and PR. If you've put in the time to create a long-form blog post, whitepaper, or industry research report, don't just publish it on your blog and call it distributed. Highlight key findings and trends, and create a guest post on a popular industry site that shares those insights. Submit it to an online publication your audience members read in order to expand the reach of your content. If you quoted someone or used their expertise, send them the finished piece and encourage them to send it to their network. (Check out our sections on social media and email marketing.)

SEO matters here, too. Every new post you add to your blog, for example, is another page that Google's going to index. More pages don't always correlate with more search traffic, but having more quality pages indexed can grant you more opportunities to rank for more search queries. If you target long-tail keywords and topics that your customers frequently search for, you should have no trouble appearing for those searches with your archive of information.

How Measurable Is It?

On a scale of 1 to 10, the measurability of content marketing is about a 5. What you can do is easily measure how your content is performing. If most of your content is web based, the backbone of tracking your progress should revolve around your web analytics tool. If you're distributing via social (which you should be) you'll be able to use that channel's metrics to see your click rates and any increases in comments, fans, and followers.

However, although likes, followers, and traffic are nice—they don't cover payroll. Before you publish a sentence, develop a set of specific key performance indicators (KPIs) that align with your business model and marketing growth channels. Track them religiously and compare them with other critical business metrics to gauge improvement. Track inbound traffic following publication, and make sure your site is set up to capitalize on those leads.

Evaluate on a regular basis whether your marketing efforts are effective or whether you need to create a new content strategy. The key items to measure include the amount of traffic, the sources of that traffic, and how long people are sticking around to read your content (time on page). There are many other metrics available, so make sure to measure key KPIs related to the concrete goals you set, and take this data into account when planning your content strategy.

How Much Does It Cost?

When it comes to content marketing the range is huge. If you want to simply tap out blog posts from your laptop late at night, the only cost is your time. But remember, a DIY strategy isn't without risks. An article or blog post can backfire if you produce your own content and don't have it vetted.

One piece did backfire for BCG Attorney Search, a legal recruiter in Pasadena, California. In 2017, founder and managing director Harrison Barnes wrote an article that appeared on the company's site and also LinkedIn, as he generally does every week. Only this piece—about why an attorney applying for a job at a firm may not hear back—was blasted for sexism, as *The American Lawyer* reported.[10] Here's the problematic section, via a version cached by Google, since the original was modified when the complaints arose:

Recruiting Coordinators Are Expected to Be Presentable, and in Many Cases They Will Be Expected to Be Attractive (Most Are in Their Early 20s to 30s)

If you have not noticed by now, most legal recruiters are women, and most are quite attractive and fit. This is because they are in positions that involve public relations—sort of like an on-air television newscaster. There is nothing wrong with the fact that most law firms put people like this in these positions because they are the public face of the law firm. What is problematical, though, is that some of these people can also—occasionally—be a little ditzy and not have the other sorts of qualifications that would make them qualified for the job. Not only do they sometimes have more beauty and fewer brains, but they also may have more beauty and less interest in people, less ability to connect with people, and similar negative characteristics. This means they expect people to treat them as if they are special and sometimes are more focused on themselves than their jobs. It is not uncommon for recruiting coordinators to use their workspaces as a hunting ground for mates—and it works. Many recruiting coordinators marry (or get married to) associates and partners inside of the law firm. This is what happens when attractive and successful people are put in confined spaces ten hours a day. Once a legal recruiting coordinator gets close to an associate or partner in the firm, the recruiting coordinator may start playing favorites—and often does. People who are close to the associate or partner may get special treatment when applying to the firm, for example. If there is tension in the job of the associate or partner (i.e., getting fired, getting a bad performance review, or leaving), this can affect the performance of the recruiting coordinator a great deal.

Barnes, as you might expect, took a lot of flak for the post. "These are not [meant to be] stereotypes," Barnes told *Inc.*'s Erik Sherman. "[All the items in the article are] observations of some things I've seen. It doesn't mean it's true about everybody." As he said, in any industry as large as law, there are going to be people who are bad at their job. "The fact that there are a few people that might be considered incompetent, that's just a fact," he said. "Honestly, I've seen far more incompetent attorneys than I've seen incompetent people in the recruiting roles."

Unfortunately, that's not how the piece read to many. Even though multiple people in the BCG office reviewed the post, as they always do, the offensive material ran. Then came the attention from the legal press, ensuring that the issue wouldn't go away.

Any time you make a remark that could be offensive to prospects or customers, you're in trouble. Remove the remark, apologize, and you may still have tainted an impression. So read, and re-read. And then have someone else read. And preferably, have an editor from outside your company read, too.

If you decide to hire a writer on your own, you may pay anywhere from a few hundred dollars per piece for someone with less experience who writes on the side, to tens of thousands to use an agency armed with an arsenal of seasoned writers and content strategists who can create and maintain a content calendar, ensure your content is top-notch, and make sure it's always aligned to your broader marketing objectives.

A Word on Video

➡ When it comes to content marketing, most companies start with articles or blog posts. But video is increasingly popular—and incredibly powerful. According to Hubspot, as of 2016, 45 percent of people watched more than an hour of Facebook or YouTube videos each week.[11]

Video is compelling and shareable—and easy for many companies to execute. *Inc.* columnist and Jamf software engineer Charles Edge suggests a series of simple steps to maximize the power of video for your business.

First, make video that's specific to your industry and true to who you are. If you have a shoe store, you can post videos about the latest hot shoe. If you have a coffee shop, you can post videos about the amazing Fair Trade coffee beans you just received. If you have a music studio, you can post video snippets of your latest soundtracks or records.

The important thing is to post authentic content that people want to watch—content that's fun—and then give viewers an easy way to find your website or otherwise engage with your product.

Once you've created great video, you've posted it (see our YouTube section in this chapter) and you've driven people to your site—what's next? You want to use those videos to push users into a sales funnel. Everything you create should have a call to action. Depending on whether the video is purely education for education's sake, or if it's designed to prime users for a product, the call to action may be "learn more" or "make an appointment" or "buy now." If you have a newsletter or post articles, embedding videos into written content can amplify your exposure to a larger audience. Give each video you make as much of a chance to gain traction as possible.

As always, rely on your analytics—but don't be a slave to vanity metrics like views and likes. If you spend all your time making videos that bring people to your site but don't actually move product, you're really only increasing your costs (web traffic and production costs) to feel cool. If you post a video and are expecting people to click on a given page but they don't, you have some incorrect assumptions. The ability to pivot in the face of what you learn is key.

INFLUENCER MARKETING

According to *AdWeek*, what others say about a brand can be up to 10 times more influential than brand-curated content.[12] Combine that with consumers' increasing distrust for traditional advertising and disingenuous marketing messages, and you have the perfect recipe for the rise of influencer marketing.

Influencer marketing is all about finding people with big social followings and working with them to convey messages about your brand or product. Think celebrity marketing, shrunk. While big companies have long been throwing money at celebrities in exchange for endorsements, today's landscape is friendlier for smaller companies. In virtually every industry, you can find influential users on Facebook, Twitter, Instagram, and Snapchat who can deliver your messages to the right consumers.

Companies have been quick to try to get a piece of the pie. In 2017, there was a more than 100 percent increase in Google searches for "influencer marketing ROI."

Getting Connected

One of the best ways to connect with known influencers in your niche is simply to build a relationship with them. This won't happen overnight, unless you're willing to pay for product endorsement. But paying is rarely a good idea: These days all audiences are wary of manufactured connections, and in particular millennials demand transparency and can smell a fake from a hundred yards away.

A more powerful type of influencer campaign is one where the person genuinely likes your product enough to sing its praises. And that leads to more followers and ultimately, sales. To make a connection, once you locate the influencers who mean something to your audience, follow their posts and engage with them, click, like, comment, and share.

True influencers are picky about the brands they partner with—because they value their relationships and treat their audiences like their best friends. "I'm careful about which brands I partner with because my audience has been built on my candor and honesty," says Emma Johnson, founder of WealthySingleMommy.com, which has 100,000 monthly unique visitors. "That is why this business works for me."

How It Works

When you work with an influencer, you have to be willing to cede some control. It isn't like an ad buy, where you control the language and the imagery. When influencers write or talk about your company or products, it has to be in their own voice—that's the whole point of working with them. Their voice gives your product credibility with their audience.

So don't expect that your influencer will hold up your product and outline its features and benefits. You can—and should—provide specific information and descriptions to ensure accuracy. But from there you have to let them be a vehicle for sharing your products in their own unique and individual way.

Most influencers will simply take the product and run with it—they know what to do. The reason you've hired an influencer in the first place is because they've managed to build up a large, engaged audience. They know how to present a product in a way that doesn't feel overly salesy and will resonate with their audience.

It can be hard for a founder to relinquish control over the message. But don't make the mistake of attempting to control the creative process. While it's important (and even necessary) to discuss your goals with the influencer, you'll find they do their best work when they have control over how they present your product.

If giving up control scares you, remember this: Most influencers will do whatever it takes to make sure you're happy and that the campaign is successful. Otherwise they've lost a customer.

Promote, Promote, Promote

While you signed up a certain influencer because they already have a significant following, do not stop there. Once the influencer has posted on your behalf, make sure you're tapping into other distribution channels, too. Repost or retweet where relevant. Post the content on your site. Plus, if the influencer has a blog or site with significant traffic, negotiate to have her create content for that as well—not just social media. Longer-form content like a blog post can be highly effective and helpful for search engine optimization, too.

Screen Your Influencers

Engaging the services of the wrong influencer can have a catastrophic impact on your brand. This is why it's vital that you properly screen anyone who will be representing your business online.

Vet the person in a similar way to a potential employee. Make sure he responds quickly to calls, emails, or texts. Look closely through his social media accounts, making sure there's no history of criticizing brands or products. Also check for controversial posts—politics, religion, or anything else you wouldn't want to be associated with your brand.

As part of your due diligence, consider screening your influencer for fake followers. While it can sound crazy, the practice of paying for fake social media followers is more common than you may think. Ask for screen shots of social media analytics that show more than just follower counts, where you can make sure your target influencer has genuine engagement from fans. If the influencer uses a newsletter, ask for open and click-through rates.

Don't Forget About Micro-Influencers

When we think of influencers, we typically think of celebrities. Household names with legions of fans, online and off. But for a startup, it may behoove you to think smaller. Micro-influencers—minor celebrities or niche bloggers—may actually have a bigger impact on your business. They may not have the huge following of a celebrity, but their audience may feel closer to them and trust them more.

These people may be hyper-connected bloggers who connect to a certain audience—think so-called "mommy bloggers" who are relied on by millions of new moms. Or they may be top industry analysts who aren't well-known outside the industry but are revered within. You know best who is best positioned within your sector or niche. So be creative when you're making your list of potential influencers for your brand.

How Much Does It Cost?

In 2017, Influence.co found that the overall average price companies paid influencers on Instagram was $271 per post.[13] But that average belies a significant point: There was a huge difference between higher-profile influencers and those with smaller followings. The average price for micro-influencers with fewer than 1,000 followers was $83 per post, while the average per-post price for influencers with more than 100,000 followers was $763.

That doesn't mean that everyone is using a pay-per-post model. Some companies pay for performance—but that can get very expensive very quickly, with no recourse. Most small companies will want to start with a safer pay-per-post approach. Some micro-influencers may even accept free products and experiences in exchange for a promotion. Obviously that's the most cost-effective option, but it'll limit your pool.

It can be hard to know what's an appropriate payment, especially if you're working with a micro-influencer. One way to try to figure it out is with tools like the Instagram Money Calculator. It will show you the estimated earnings per post for different influencers. Just enter their Instagram username. The tool makes its calculations based on the number of followers and the engagement rate of recent posts.

Instant Pot
Courts Home Chefs

IN 2016, AMAZON TOUTED the success of its second annual Prime Day promotion in a press release, rattling off how much stuff people bought in different categories:

- 90,000 televisions

- 2 million toys

- 1 million pairs of shoes

- 200,000 headphones

- 215,000 Instant Pot 7-in-1 Multi-Functional Pressure Cookers

One of those lines stands out—the very specific mention of pressure cookers. It's one of the only products mentioned by brand name, in a sea of broader categories ("headphones," and "pairs of shoes"). Here's how it happened.[14]

The Instant Pot is a product of a small Canadian company with 25 employees and no traditional advertising. Micro-influencers have long been a part of the company's marketing strategy. Over the last seven years, since it first hit the market, the company "has provided free Instant Pots to 200 bloggers and cookbook authors who represent many styles of cooking, including Chinese, Italian, sous vide, and vegan," according to NPR.[15] Company CEO Robert Wang has noted in interview after interview that his goal has always been to use self-generated recommendations to build buzz among an engaged audience of home chefs.

It has worked. The device earned a cult following after Amazon ran a promotion, resulting in 215,000-plus sales in one day, along with rabid word-of-mouth buzz. Today, enthusiasts trade recipe hacks and videos in a 450,000-member Instant Pot Facebook group.

Even with the appliance ranking among Amazon's top-selling kitchen products in the U.S., Wang claims to still read every Amazon review. He says they provide clues for designing new features, like the fourth-generation model's Bluetooth connectivity, which adjusts cooking time according to a user's altitude.

—

That will give you a rough idea how much you may end up paying, depending on the reach of the influencers you're considering.

Entrepreneur John Rampton, who says his early forays into influencer marketing weren't nearly as successful as they could have been, recommends spending no more than 50 percent of your social media advertising budget. So, if you have $5,000 to spend on social media, you should be investing no more than $2,500 on influencers who can promote you on a variety of platforms.

How Measurable Is It?

Numbers range across studies but the return on investment for influencer marketing has in some cases been found to be more than $7 for every $1 spent. That certainly explains the current frenzy around it—but it doesn't mean it's a guarantee.

Once you have an idea of the prices you're likely to be facing, you may want to consider a test, especially if you're working with multiple influencers or on more than one channel. Start with a test budget—it'll depend on your payment amount, but maybe a few thousand dollars—and figure out how funds will need to be allocated. A majority of your budget will go to paying your influencers. But you may need to allocate funds for influencer marketing tools, any paid marketing you're putting against the campaign, or any other elements like contests or promotions.

Don't assume that just because an influencer promotes your product x number of times to x number of people, the campaign is "successful." Monitor performance closely. Try tracking:

→ Referral traffic

→ Increase in your own social media following

→ Links acquired

→ Qualified leads

→ Revenue/conversions from campaign

→ Shares of campaign

If any of the influencers are underperforming, you can choose to exclude them from the next campaign. Once you see how things are going, you may want to build in an incentive for performance for your top influencer partners.

6

TAKING IT OFFLINE

DIRECT MAIL

Direct mail is just what it sounds like: sending messages to target customers through the mail. Postcards, mailers, catalogs.

Sounds a bit quaint, right? At one time, direct mail was a particularly attractive option for small business owners. It can communicate complete information about a product or service and reach almost any conceivable target group, all for a relatively low cost.

It seems so analog. With text messages, Facebook messages, tweets, and Instagram—not to mention good, old-fashioned email— why would anyone use the post office to reach out to customers? Depending on what you're trying to accomplish, it can be surprisingly effective.

Let's start with the response rate for unsolicited messages. When it comes to direct mail, anything from 0.5 to 2 percent may be considered a solid response rate. In some cases, response rates can reach 5 percent or more when you use a "house list" of existing customers and opt-in recipients, according to the Direct Marketing Association's 2016 Response Rate Report. That's dramatically higher than email marketing, where a 0.01 percent response rate is considered solid.

Plus, research shows that physical media, such as a paper letter, postcard, or flyer, leaves a greater impression on the brain than electronic media does—not surprising in an increasingly cluttered digital world. There's also a higher chance it will stand out from the crowd since people get less snail mail—and more email—than ever before.

There are certain situations where direct mail is particularly effective:

You Want to Reach High-Level Decisionmakers

Email marketing to this demographic virtually never works, since they have tight spam filters and often human gatekeepers who clean out their inboxes. A direct mail piece that looks like business correspondence may have a better shot of landing on their desks.

You're Introducing Yourself

New to the neighborhood, or the industry? A direct mail piece is a great way to grab people's attention in a crowded marketplace. An oversized postcard with compelling graphics might just catch their eye when an online ad or unsolicited email would be ignored.

You Want Precise Targeting

It sounds counterintuitive, but it is possible to target pretty tightly when you use direct mail. When you buy a list, investigate how it can be sliced up. You can target by zip code, profession, or by association membership, for example. Use your personas to create direct mail campaigns targeted tightly to those people.

That can help you save on costs as well. If tight targeting has produced a list of only a hundred people who truly fit your target customer profile, and your direct mail item costs $0.65 apiece, you can reach that target market for only $65 plus the cost of buying the list.

You're Promoting a Holiday or Event

Direct mail is an especially good way to get the word out and customers through the door when you're running a promotion that ties in with an event such as a sporting match or a holiday. You don't have to have a product or service that's overtly related; you just need to be able to draw a connection. Think a landscaping service targeting high-end homes around Arbor Day, or a meal delivery service targeting working moms on Labor Day—which happens to correspond to the busy back-to-school season.

You Want People to Take an Action

While direct mail is a great way to earn eyeballs and attention, it's not as useful for straight-through selling: You can't link to a product page from a direct mail piece like you can with an email. This is why your direct mail marketing should have a strong call to action, which in most cases will be to send people to your website for more information, to receive a discount, or to download a free piece of content. You want to use the direct mail to generate interest and ideally, to create a warm lead.

Kopari Beauty Catches Eyes

BRYCE GOLDMAN AND JAMES Brennan know a thing or two about what it takes to look good. The co-founders of Kopari Beauty, a San Diego-based skin care product maker, have been using direct mail for years because, even though it is more expensive than email, it has unbeatable stopping power.

A typical mailing would consist of 25,000 two-sided color mailings. "It's about catching their eye," Brennan says. Kopari's mail pieces, he adds, "are looking to make conversions and sales, but it's just as important to make impressions."

They've gotten pretty good at both: The company gets a response rate of 2.5 to 3 percent, triple the national average of the standard email campaign.

How Much Does It Cost?

All that postage and paper means it can cost more than twice as much to get a customer response as it does for an email campaign. Besides the postage and printing, you need to have the pieces designed and written, and possibly pay for a mailing list. Altogether, depending on the size and weight of your piece, you may end up paying anywhere from $0.50 per piece to a few dollars for something like a catalog.

What would you do with $10,000 for marketing?

> Direct mail—it's a hidden gem. Everybody thinks it's old school; nobody focuses on it anymore, which provides more opportunity for those of us who do. People who open up mail are a specific demographic. If your product fits in with the responsible, middle-aged group who typically open their mail, direct mail can be huge."

JIM CARLSON, CEO, *Zurixx*

Can I DIY?

You can handle all of these tasks yourself, you can outsource some of them—for instance just the sorting and mailing—or you can find a vendor to take on the whole process. Outsourcing your mailings to a specialist shop means you won't need to study postal regulations, mailing-list composition, or what's ominously called "list hygiene." Direct mail must be sorted by ZIP code and route, and doing that "improperly might cost an additional two pennies per piece," says Brian Johnson, founder of Mail Shark, a direct mail services company.

Creating Mail That Works

To capture a consumer's fleeting attention and avoid being tossed into the garbage bin, direct mail needs to check a few boxes.

First, your pictures are crucial for maximizing direct mail's "trust factor," says Joy Gendusa, CEO of marketing company Postcard Mania. "With B2B mailings, for example, I always recommend that there be a photo of some person at the company on the card," she says. "That just makes it real, instead of a stock photo." Passport Health, which operates more than 250 travel-immunization clinics around North America, has successfully used postcards that feature exotic animals. In a recent spring, a postcard campaign increased the rate of customers seeking booster shots by 10 to 14 percent in the first month, according to Vicki Sowards, Passport's director of nursing resources.

Next, decide what you want customers or potential customers to do.

"Our company sends out over 100,000 direct mail pieces per month. We love that direct mail busts through the clutter of an inbox and can become a billboard on your prospect's refrigerator," said Todd Toback, CEO of Get It Done House Buyers, a volume home-buying company. Direct mail campaigns can generate phone calls and leads; for his company, it's used to follow up with prospects to help close deals. Depending on how your marketing is structured, you may want customers to call, or to visit your company's Facebook page. "In our experience, direct mail often starts the conversation, and the Internet helps us close it," Toback says.

"Multiple touches take credibility through the roof, differentiating you from competitors."

If you want customers to buy something, be aggressive. "Business owners will pick a wimpy offer, something that doesn't cost them a lot of money," says Steven Wagner, owner of the postcard mailer Health Media Concepts. "You've got to break through the clutter, or you're going to waste your money." So instead of a 10 percent discount, offer a substantial freebie—an important report, a product sample, or even a tote bag—to make an impression.

What About ROI?

When done right, the return on investment is surprising, say founders who have come to rely on direct mail as a powerful tool in their marketing arsenal.

As the marketing manager of Fox's Pizza Den, a family-owned franchise business spanning twenty-five states, Adam Haupricht mails 500,000 promotional postcards at a time. The campaigns cost 25 cents per piece including postage, and Haupricht says he's seen new stores increase sales as much as 30 to 40 percent over thirty weeks using them. Keeping it fresh is the key, he says. "A generic postcard with the same old coupons on the back—no menu, nothing fancy—is the least effective," Haupricht says. He talks to the owners of the company's 250 franchises about ideas for each new mailing. "I say, 'Hey, what do you want to try? What's working? What's not?'"

Sometimes, effectiveness can be measured by a single response. That's what happened in 2014, recalls entrepreneur Brian Roberts, when he was stuck.

"My goal was to get my former fashion accessories brand into Urban Outfitters. We had just landed several major media features, but the coverage got the attention of everyone but my intended target: their accessories buyers," Roberts says.

Since he couldn't get them to reach out to him, he had no choice but to reach out to them. He knew he'd never break through the email clutter. Phone calls just aren't viable for a visual product like accessories. "I needed a different way to reach out that wouldn't result in me getting lost in the pile."

He typed up a letter and ordered several custom postcards and catalogs from an online printing company based in California. Less than a month after sending the mailing, he says, he got a call from a buyer who liked a few styles in the catalog. Shortly after that sit down, the brand was picked up by Urban Outfitters.

 ## How Measurable Is It?

Direct mail is extremely testable. You can try out different sales messages on various audiences in order to find the most profitable market for a new product or service. Using consumer data from providers like Experian, you can target your direct mail to your ideal market, and then link responses to individual customers' social media accounts, email addresses, and mobile phones.

TV

These days most small businesses focus on digital rather than TV, and they're in good company: In 2016, digital advertising sales overtook TV advertising for the first time ever, according to *AdAge*.[1]

If you're like many entrepreneurs, you may view TV as too expensive and may believe that only large national companies can advertise there. While that may have been true a generation ago, the advent of cable television and the explosion of stations and programming has made TV an advertising medium that can be effective for even local businesses—somewhat surprisingly, it's a medium that businesses of virtually any size can afford.

For certain types of small or mid-sized businesses, television may be a better advertising medium than any other. If your product is visual, for example, TV may make a lot of sense. "If you're a local firm, such as a jeweler, you don't need to run ads nationally," says J. T. Hroncich, managing director of Capitol Media Solutions, an agency that helps companies buy advertising. "Cable TV is very reasonable. As opposed to taking out an ad during *American Idol* on broadcast TV, you can take out a local ad on a popular cable show, such as *Top Chef.* It all depends on who your target market is."

What's more, TV still has a certain cachet, and can signal to a certain market that you're for real, making it appealing to businesses that are looking for a strong branding play or trying to boost name recognition. Plus, if you have a clear target audience, and you know they're watching something, it can be an effective tactic. Just take DraftKings and FanDuel, two of the biggest startups in fantasy sports. The two companies spent hundreds of millions on TV ads during the 2015 football season—ads that aired during games, when they knew their target market would be glued to their couches.

Expensive? Often. But it doesn't have to be.

 ## How Much Does It Cost?

Before jumping in, you need to understand your budget for advertising. Be sure to include the costs associated with producing your commercial. You can produce your ad independently or with a television station, but costs can vary wildly. "It really depends on what you want," Hroncich says. "If you're a family-run business and you want to film a thirty-second spot that shows a screen shot of your dinner special, it's not going to be very costly. But if there are actors employed, that will cost you more."

Then there is the cost of the advertising campaign. You typically don't want to spend your advertising budget all at once. You want to air it with a bit of frequency so that people will see it a number of times and it reaches a larger percentage of your target market. Typically, television stations will accept spot lengths of ten, fifteen, thirty, and sixty seconds—but the good news is, shorter commercials are becoming the norm: Fifteen seconds is increasingly common.

Options for advertising on TV include national networks, which reach a national audience; local broadcast or independent stations, which reach a regional or local market; and cable television, which can be national, regional, or local. If you cater to a specific demographic, consider niche cable channels that may have lower numbers of viewers overall—but those viewers may be a strong match for your products or services.

With all of those variables, costs can vary widely. If you can self-produce, and your fifteen-second ad is going to run locally, you may only spend a few thousand dollars, all in. (Though note that local markets like New York and Los Angeles will cost dramatically more than smaller cities.) Contrast that with a national, prime-time ad, which can run into the hundreds of thousands. According to *Ad-Age*, the average cost of a commercial during a recent season of *The Walking Dead* was $400,000. Keep in mind, too, that rates will vary depending on timing and seasonality—rates tend to rise when anticipated hot new shows premiere, or when a closely watched election is on the horizon.

Make It Local

→ The best local ads target not the faceless millions but actual customers and neighbors. They deepen the sense of community identity. "When you are in the community, these ad campaigns draw on a set of shared references" that everyone recognizes, says Melody Warnick, author of the book, *This Is Where You Belong: The Art and Science of Loving the Place You Live*. The ads also "create new references as people talk about them, and those become part of the city's narrative," says Warnick. "Everyone has seen them and can laugh about them together."

Finding a Bargain

There are ways to get a commercial on the air more cheaply than the advertised rate.

→ **Pay up front.** Station sales reps love it when their income stream is secure, and they'll work hard for you as a result.

→ **Commit to a multiple-week schedule.** Most cost-efficient packages are sold on a ten- to thirteen-week basis, and stations would rather have spots booked in advance, to help manage their inventory and plan against it. If you work through a cable company that has many different stations, you might be able to strike up multiple-week deals on a variety of programs. You may be able to plan for weekend placement that runs across different programming types, for example, if that's important for your target market.

→ **Take advantage of market conditions.** If the local economy is slowing, chances are the airtime available on local television stations is aplenty and you can negotiate some terrific deals.

→ **Look for fire sales.** It doesn't happen often, but if stations have excess slots because of local or national advertising conditions, it presents an opportunity for small businesses. Quite often, they will include programming you would otherwise not be able to afford.

→ **Participate in auctions.** When you purchase advertising via an auction, you will need to pay up front, and may not have a clear understanding of what time slots you'll be receiving. Because of the uncertainty, rather than base your entire television schedule on auctions, you may want to use the auction to complement your schedule.

→ **Buy remnants.** You can purchase inexpensive remnant packages with a range of flexibility; the more flexible you are, the more savings you will receive. A remnant package generally puts you on a kind of "auto-fill" schedule, where your ads might appear just about any time, on any day of the week. That can feel risky, but you may end up scoring a placement during a popular show that can easily pay for the package.

→ **Negotiate added value.** When booking airtime, you can almost always negotiate for extras or "a value add," Hroncich says. "We did a cable TV buy for one of our clients recently and we got some free advertising on their website as a value add and some public service announcements at no charge." PSAs are ten-second spots to air when available during your flight (the schedule of advertising for a period of time). Hroncich notes that advertising agencies can often help negotiate these value add deals better because they're aware of what the stations have offered other advertisers in the past.

→ **Negotiate a media mix.** Ask if the television station has a website and see if there are any potential promotional activities on that website if you buy TV advertising. Maybe your ad can run on-site or maybe you can create a corresponding banner.

How Measurable Is It?

It's tough. You can measure visits to your website after your commercial airs, or look for a sales boost. But specific, detailed metrics are nearly impossible to collect.

Can I DIY?

When it comes to producing your commercial, DIY is a tough path to go down. It takes a certain amount of expertise—not to mention equipment—to script, direct, and shoot a commercial, no matter how short. A freelance TV producer may be able to help for an hourly rate. Or your local TV stations may offer their own in-house production services for a relatively low cost.

RADIO

Though it's one of the oldest forms of mass media still in use, radio remains a useful and profitable tool for marketers. According to a recent study from Nielsen, 59 percent of U.S. music listeners listen to traditional or online radio.[2]

Even in the digital age, radio offers certain unique advantages. It remains the best way to reach consumers as they commute, giving it a leg up for certain local businesses. "It is still really relevant, but a lot depends on the market. If you're in Atlanta, Washington, D.C., or Los Angeles, where a lot of people still drive to work, it's a good platform to get your advertising message out," says Capitol Media Solutions' Hroncich.

Over and over, studies show that radio remains effective for marketers. In 2014, Nielsen reported that radio ads drive 5.8 percent of U.S. retail sales.[3] Considering that more ad dollars are spent on TV, Internet, and print ads than on radio ads, 5.8 percent represents a pretty good return on investment. Put another way, each dollar of radio ad spend generates an average sales return of $6—though returns tend to be higher for local businesses like retail stores rather than national products.

How Much Does It Cost?

Like TV, your cost will vary based on the size of the market you're advertising to. You may pay as little as fifteen dollars per play for a thirty-second ad in a small city market, or a few hundred dollars per play in a large one. Contracts are often available so you're paying a flat fee for a certain number of plays over the course of a month.

Often, radio stations will help produce the commercial for you as part of an advertising deal. You generally can give them copy and they'll create the ad. That may be included in the price, or you may pay an additional fee: Find out before you sign the contract.

Radio stations will also often offer package deals that include banner advertising on their website or mentions in newsletters they send. Those options may add a few thousand dollars to your advertising package. Pricier options may include a popular DJ endorsing your product or the sponsorship of a local event.

Getting a Bargain

Just like TV, you can save by planning ahead and committing to the long term—often thirteen to twenty-six weeks. Plus, generally your rate will be guaranteed, even if there are rate increases.

If you don't purchase your radio campaign in advance, you are at the mercy of supply and demand, and rates may increase as inventory decreases. You may not be able to run your campaign at all if a station is sold out during busy months.

"Negotiation is key. You have to go in and negotiate what you want," says Hroncich. "There's a lot more to it than placing a simple print ad. You have to look at the target audience you're looking to reach, the size of your budget, and the ratings of the stations you are interested in purchasing."

Get Creative

Radio broadcasters are open to creative arrangements such as bartering for airtime, says Tara Hartley, an advertising consultant. In one deal she put together, for example, a client swapped $250,000 worth of excess retail inventory for $100,000 worth of radio advertising over a four-year period. The station used the goods for listener giveaways as well as for in-house sales incentives. "In broadcast—radio and TV—there are all kinds of opportunities to go beyond the rate card," she says, including free bonus spots, or commercials that use the on-air talent to endorse a product, which has the added benefit of getting union-mandated actor fees waived.

Consider the Rotator

Run of station (ROS) commercials, otherwise known as rotator spots, are lower-priced commercials with a broad window of airtime—although there are usually no guarantees when your commercial will air. The most popular, and thus most expensive, times to run radio ads are during the morning and afternoon "drive time"—the rush hours, when lots of listeners are commuting. But an ROS commercial may air anytime from 6:00 a.m. to midnight. If a station happens to have availability, you may be able to get that lower ROS rate for high-demand times, but it doesn't happen often. One strategy to consider is to purchase some guaranteed times and supplement those airplays with rotators.

Fringe days or times are when ads are less in demand, or not as highly rated as other time slots, and are priced accordingly. Consider midday, evenings, or weekends, when rates on many stations are less expensive than during weekday drive times.

Buy a Remnant

Like TV, remnant packages are available if you're flexible about when your ad airs. Natalie Hale, CEO of Media Partners Worldwide, a radio remnant dealer based in California, says in the Los Angeles market she can get a sixty-second spot that normally goes for $300 for somewhere around $50. But those discounts aren't for everybody. Hale says she won't work with a client unless they're willing to spend at least $5,000 to $10,000 per week.

 ### Can I DIY?

Probably. Radio stations target local businesses and have the infrastructure to help get your ad produced. You will, though, need to do the legwork to make sure your audience lines up with the station's. Advertising agencies are often hired to do the research and the bidding for you, and can often negotiate more "value added" features to a contract.

How Measurable Is It?

Like TV, it's tough. You can measure visits to your website after your commercial airs, or look for a sales boost if you advertise a time-sensitive promotion. But specific, detailed metrics are nearly impossible to collect.

OUT-OF-HOME

Plastering your startup on a billboard may not be the first thing you think of when it comes to advertising in the twenty-first century, but for some businesses, it can be quite effective. Placing small billboards in novel or unexpected locations can be a smart way for cash-strapped businesses to stand out in a world increasingly cluttered with ads. One reason out-of-home ads can be more effective than other forms of advertising, such as TV commercials, is that they often have a captive audience that can't simply change the channel or head to the kitchen for a snack. That's why consumers are more likely to remember ads placed in venues like sports arenas and bowling alleys than those that appear on television—they're staring at that ad for an extended period of time, and may be absorbing its contents without even realizing.

What's more, people who are already on the go are more likely to stop off at a new restaurant or shop than those who are already in their robes and slippers—making strategic out-of-home ad placement smart for local or neighborhood-driven businesses.

Take the famous "Got Milk?" campaign, which lasted an astonishing twenty years before being retired in 2014. Media planners bought billboard space near grocery stores and convenience shops—a timely reminder for shoppers and passersby who were inspired to pick up a gallon on their way home from work or school.

Highway or local billboards aren't the only option. If your target is an urban market, like New York, Washington, D.C., or Chicago, subway ads may fit the bill. If you have a B2B product, think airport advertising. Revisit your customer profile and figure out where they go and what their needs are at that time.

"People coming home from work around 6:00 p.m. are hungry and very susceptible to our message," says Matt Maloney, founder and CEO of online food delivery company Grubhub. "We figured this out when we advertised on mass transit in Chicago. We had noticed that the person managing the outdoor ads was really bad at taking them down, so we knew if we bought a month of space, we'd get five. That placement worked very well. It has been a staple of our advertising ever since."

While billboards are about as old school as you can get, projecting a static piece of marketing to a crowd, new technology is changing that. The technology is called targeted Digital Out of Home (DOOH). It can capture smartphone IDs, which are then matched to existing advertising IDs that catalogue online search and social media data. The result is an immediate profile of a whole crowd.

That means that if a particular crowd is comprised of college students, or high-net-worth dads, or Spanish-speaking professionals, the signs will serve up an ad that's targeted to that audience. That doesn't mean that billboards will suddenly begin to serve ads based on your specific profile, but it will aggregate your profile along with the rest of the crowd, coming up with messaging that's tailored to a certain demographic, offering a huge new potential opportunity for this old-school medium.

Speaking of old school, if the majority of your business is done locally, don't overlook one of the oldest out-of-home tactics around:

Leaving flyers around town is a nearly free way—you just pay for the printing—to drum up awareness. Handing them out in person is even better, and it gives you an opportunity to tell people about your company and give them a face to connect it with. Flyers are especially important if your business is new and you know the market exists, but you're having trouble tapping into it.

How Much Does It Cost?

Highway billboards may cost as little as $1,000 for a four-week period, or as much as $15,000, depending on the size, the location, and the number of impressions the ad is likely to get.

In New York City, your startup can cover the interior of an entire subway train for about $17,000 a month (the industry calls this a "spectacular"), or an entire subway station. Your startup can also own every commercial image in an entire station, like the busy Columbus Circle subway station, which costs about $200,000 a month.

Can I DIY?

You can. But a marketing agency can help on two fronts. First, they will have expertise in negotiating out-of-home contracts, which can be hugely helpful if you're navigating a complex market like New York City or you're looking for national exposure. An agency can also help you craft the most compelling creative possible. With just a few seconds to grab consumers' interest, it can be surprisingly tough to craft a message that's simple—ideally fewer than ten words—and easy to digest and remember.

Steven Singer
Invents an In Joke

DRIVING DOWN I-95, NONRESIDENTS of the Philadelphia-New Jersey-Delaware region may do a double take. The billboard is black. Scrawled across it in angry white capital letters is the simple message "I HATE STEVEN SINGER."

Any local will tell you that Singer is the owner of a self-named jewelry shop in Center City, Philadelphia, who has reveled in hate for nearly two decades. Around here, the story is legend. Around 1999, a man bought his wife a Steven Singer diamond ring to celebrate their twentieth anniversary. Nine months later, he returned with a newborn baby and some loud invective about the business he blamed for his unplanned, late-in-life fatherhood. A delighted Singer thought the contrarian message of hate would stand out in an industry soggy with declarations of love.

At first "none of the radio or billboard companies would take our ad," says Singer, who opened his store in 1980. "When one of the radio companies did, it made me pay in advance, even though I had been advertising with them for a decade. They thought we were going to go out of business so fast they might never get paid."

Singer started with one billboard to make it seem like the work of a single irate customer. (Today, he typically has 10 or 20 billboards at a time.) The first radio ad featured the guy who inspired the campaign telling his story. In a bit of luck, that guy happened to be Dennis Steele, recognized by locals as the actor who does ads for the Phillies, the Pennsylvania Lottery, and the *Philadelphia Inquirer* newspaper. Steele remains the company's voice.

Over the years, Singer has changed up the campaign with different haters and motivations. Husbands hate Steven Singer because their spouses get angry when they offer anything other than one of Singer's diamonds as a gift. National competitors (Singer names them on the billboards) supposedly seethe when Steven Singer beats them on price.

The campaign, says Singer, has a very local attitude. "It's representative of the atmosphere and the climate in Philly," he says. "The working man, Rocky kind of thing. If you are looking for Tiffany's, we're not that."

And locals love being in on the joke. Every time Singer passes through the airport or takes out his credit card, people gleefully inform him of their animus. Philadelphia Mayor Jim Kenney once interrupted a speech he was giving before the local Chamber of Commerce to announce, "I hate Steven Singer," after noticing the jeweler sitting on the dais. "Everyone thinks they are the first to say it, but I hear it fifty to a hundred times a day," says Singer. "I love it."

—

How Measurable Is It?

Not very. A company could have a unique phone number or URL on a billboard, or even a special offer, but it would be hard to figure the true number of "generated actions" that resulted from it. Even if you're asking customers whether they saw the billboard or what brought them in, you can't always count on their answers. Many may mention modes of marketing your business doesn't use. So, while it's worth asking, bank on this question providing utterly skewed ROI statistics.

In some cases, out-of-home can be a powerful form of branding—albeit one without a measurable return. When email marketing company MailChimp took out billboards, they offered no keywords or calls to action. Instead, early billboards simply depicted the company's monkey mascot, winking at passersby. More recently, MailChimp has used its Atlanta billboards as giant canvasses that feature the work of local artists. They may not be able to directly track sales to the strategy, but when it comes to positive brand sentiment, the results are priceless.

OTHER OLD-SCHOOL ADVERTISING

While you don't hear much about it these days, buying print ads in newspapers or magazines is still a viable strategy for some businesses. Ad prices have come down in recent years, and most small businesses start out buying print ads in their local, neighborhood newsweeklies. But that's no longer necessarily the only safe option. Another smart way to get your feet wet in print advertising is to buy remnant space available through different dealers. Like on radio or TV, remnant space is the ad industry's equivalent of last-minute super-savers; publications with an extra page or two to fill will sell it off at a much lower price. This has become more common as newspaper ad sales have plummeted over the last decade.

An ad in a newspaper may range anywhere from a few hundred dollars for a quarter-page in a small-circulation paper to several thousand for a paper in a large market. While few startups would rely solely on newspaper ads these days, they can be an effective strategy if you're trying to reach a local audience at a certain time— for example, to advertise a time-sensitive promotion or event.

NO MATTER WHERE
YOU'RE ADVERTISING . . . REMEMBER

You need to have a clear understanding of what it is that you want to accomplish with your ads. Make sure that you write these goals down: They should govern the decisions you make with your ads. Do you want new customers? How many? Do you want more visits to your website? Are you looking to get people to register for your event? The more specific you are with your goals, the more you can tailor your ads to help you reach your goals, and the more you can track your progress to make necessary tweaks to your ads.

EVENT MARKETING

Hosting a company event can be powerful marketing: You meet potential customers face-to-face, demonstrate your expertise or cachet in the market, and engage them. But events can end up expensive cocktail parties if they're not done right. You need to make sure there's significant consumer engagement long after the event is over.

"What people do wrong is they don't have a clear objective," says Tres McCullough, co-founder of Fathom, an experiential marketing firm based in New York City that has done events for clients like LG and Gatorade. "A lot of companies have a great idea, everything is watertight and clear, and they race to execution mode. The event engages the client base, goes off without a hitch. Then it's gone."

The key is to identify a measurable goal that everything is geared toward accomplishing. "Anyone can throw a great party, but this isn't about throwing a great party. It's about hitting business objectives," McCullough says.

Decide Your Objective

Start by asking yourself precisely why you're hosting the event, says Audrey Shedivy, founder of Henry Grey PR, a public relations firm and marketing boutique based in Chicago. She has coordinated events ranging from small gatherings to a Rodeo Drive store launch. According to a 2011 survey from *BtoB* magazine and marketing company Marketo, 83 percent of companies want to generate leads from their events. But that's not the only goal many companies have. Seventy-two percent are looking for increased customer engagement, and an equal number are looking to build their brand.[4]

"Are you hosting the event to thank your existing customers and attract new ones? Are you launching a new product and want to create buzz among influencers?" Shedivy poses. "Whatever your goal for the event, identify that up front. It will help guide your decisions in planning the event." If your goal is to deepen relationships with existing customers, you may want to plan a series of small workshops around the country, for example. But if your main objective is branding, you may plan a single, large event with high-profile keynote speakers who drum up lots of outside interest.

Create a Guest List

To get people interested, you need to give them a reason to show up. "This is where you can really get creative," Shedivy says. "The draw for your event could be its location, such as a new hot spot in town that people are eager to check out, or it could be the entertainment you've hired if you have access to a recognized artist. New product launches and pop-up openings are a draw in and of themselves, as people are excited to be the first to see something cool."

How you draw people in will differ depending on the type of business and type of event. Rebecca and Uri Minkoff, co-founders of the Rebecca Minkoff fashion brand, faced a changing retail environment, with more transactions happening online. So they turned a store into a destination, hosting eight yoga classes a day for a week, hosted by a well-known New York yoga studio, at the same time the brand was launching an athleisure line of apparel and opening a new store in Los Angeles. The classes "created so much word of mouth and goodwill," Rebecca Minkoff says—and boosted sales both in the store and online, as word spread through social media.

Any successful event, no matter the type, requires a good turnout, Shedivy says. "Build your guest list keeping in mind the big picture goal for your event," she says. "Request that invitees RSVP. It makes your event feel more special and it will help you keep a handle on how many people to expect. Unless you know your guests very well and are certain they will all show up, assume that about 40 percent of those who RSVP won't show up."

Make sure you have time to generate enough buzz—about six months is generally safe. The speakers you have at your event are ultimately what generates your audience, and the good ones book up fast. You need to be able to plan around their schedules. Also, your attendees need to plan their travel schedule. The sooner you can start spreading the word, the better your turnout.

If your event relies on recruiting big-name speakers, offer ways to help them achieve their goals to encourage them to sign on. Give them dedicated space at the event, create Q&A sessions, "fireside chats," private meet and greets or a special photo opportunity where your audience gets a chance to connect with the speakers. Maybe a few select attendees have a private dinner with the keynote speaker.

As you nail down the standout features of the event, don't forget to consider basic logistics. Your ideal date and time will be determined by your target attendees. Thursday evenings tend to be popular for professionals, while breakfasts or lunches work well for stay-at-home parents. Make sure you know your target market's weekly routine so you're catering to them.

Generate Buzz

Once you have your speakers locked in, start running targeted social media ads that are shown to your ideal audience. Focus your ad sets on people who are already following your speakers because some of those fans will be eager to see their idols live.

You can also target your ad sets to show to people who live in the area where your event is taking place. Facebook and other channels' detailed targeting options allow you to show the ads precisely to people in the area, even down to the zip code.

Ask your own community to spread the word about your event. You can set up a private Facebook group or use a dedicated hashtag. Attendees will be able to network with one another, creating both buzz and an advantage for them.

Incentivize your speakers and other promotional partners to promote your event. For example, you might ask them to email their customers and offer them a chance to give away a handful of tickets for free or incentivize it with a discount code. That way, their followers will get an exclusive deal, making them feel even more special, and you'll generate more buzz for your event. You can also do Facebook livestream interviews or Snapchat story swaps with those who have a relevant following.

The more you focus your marketing efforts around building a community and making your audience feel special, the more you'll create "ambassadors" who will help you market your event through word of mouth. Just be aware that your job is not over once you've gotten everyone to turn up to the event. You want to truly add value to the businesses of your attendees, so that they continue to show up year after year—and bring their friends.

Make the Most of Your Invitees

If you're hosting an event to drive leads, make sure not to keep all of your focus on the event itself. It's important, sure, but so are the opportunities surrounding the event—from the save the date to the reminder email and post-event follow-up. Businesses that are strategic about these touch points do much better than those who just focus on the event itself.

That includes not forgetting about your attendees as the weeks and months go by. Continue engaging with them throughout the year by creating special contests and activities. Once the group grows into a tight-knit community, they'll happily share upcoming events with their friends and on their social media pages. And don't exclude those who RSVPed but didn't make it to the event. Things come up, and it's normal to have more than a third of planned attendees not make it. That doesn't mean they're not interested, so keep them engaged.

How Much Does It Cost?

The cost varies dramatically based on the type of event. A bagel-and-coffee breakfast at your office will cost you thousands less than a cocktail party at a hot restaurant. Somewhere in between the two is a lunch-and-learn session at a local university club or similar venue.

When it comes to speakers, some lesser-known ones will participate as long as travel expenses are covered, while others command speaking fees that can reach into the five figures.

If you elect to invest in a well-known keynote speaker, make sure you take advantage of the time that you have her. Record a short video interview or podcast for your website, or if she's an author, ask her to sign books that you can use as part of a promotion or incentive. Remember that high-profile speakers often have large social networks; if they agree to spread the word about your event, the investment can pay off in dividends.

And don't forget the cost of marketing. Spreading the word through your already existing channels is free. But if you plan to send printed invitations, or advertise via promoted social media posts, incorporate those costs into your projections.

Can I Measure It?

Often. It depends on the objective of your event and how well you track outcomes. You may land a client as a direct result of an in-person networking session, or close a deal with a key supplier. You may add dozens of new subscribers to your newsletter, which is a significant starting point for your sales funnel.

Sometimes the ROI from an event is the unexpected or perhaps, a secondary goal. A company throws a recruiting event, and inadvertently closes its biggest deal of the year. A tech company hosts a networking event to drive sales leads, and ends up hiring two of their best employees. That's the beauty of events—you can track more than one key performance indicator. Just make sure you have an infrastructure in place to collect information and track every opportunity that comes up from your event, including those you weren't anticipating.

Can I DIY?

The planning and details necessary to pull off even modestly sized events can be daunting. Before you commit to a let's-roll-up-our-sleeves event marketing mentality, do a little homework on event planning companies in your area. You can decide whether you need your event solutions provider to take charge or be a part of the ranks depending upon your budget.

An event planner may charge an hourly fee, or he may charge a percentage of the total event cost. Either way, unless the event is very small, you'll be spending thousands of dollars. Event planning can be excruciatingly detailed—think decisions about whether 2 percent milk or skim should be served with the coffee—and time consuming. The upshot of outsourcing event planning is that you'll have fewer challenges along the way, leaving you maximum time to concentrate on your business objectives.

MAKING THE MOST OF A TRADE SHOW

A trade show offers a rare platform where you can market and sell in the same place: You're given the advantage of knowing that just about everyone you speak to will have an interest in or use for what you sell. While typically marketing is a first step and a way to direct a potential customer to your website or store, at a trade show you are marketing to someone who could immediately turn into a sale. Since a good majority of the sales process can be done right then and there, for most business types, the funnel from first exposure to purchase is much shorter. Shorter lead nurturing means more sales.

That doesn't mean you can just show up with a flashy display and call it a day. Trade shows are expensive, exhausting, and intense. Get the most from your investment: Set measurable objectives before the event and stick to them.

Start Before the Show

"People have this idea that a successful trade show is one where you have 10,000 people walking past your booth," says Malcolm Gilvar, executive vice president of sales for the Trade Group, a trade show design and consulting service. "But that can be a barrier to your success." Getting the right kind of traffic to your booth starts before the trade show with pre-show activity such as email blasts or marketing campaigns. "Define who you want to come to your exhibit and target them specifically," Gilvar continues. "If people did nothing but that, it would be an amazingly successful event."

Think One Person at a Time

Trade shows offer you a natural way to forge a connection, since your customer is able to put a face to your name and isn't dealing with just another voice on the other end of the phone. Make the most of it. When an attendee approaches you, you know you have their undivided attention and the opportunity to educate them in a way you don't usually have: You have your target audience right in front of you. If you use your time with them wisely, you could not only introduce them to your product or service but also educate them on what makes your company different and why they should do business with you.

Don't underestimate the power of good old-fashioned connections. When *Inc.* columnist John Brandon attends the huge CES event each year in Las Vegas, there's one tried-and-true method that seems to work best—a method that far too few companies employ. "As I would walk down the hallway, sometimes a person approached me and asked a few quick basic questions. How was the show going for me so far? Was I a member of the media? Did I have a few minutes to see a new product?" Brandon wrote on Inc.com "The reason this worked is that everyone has a desire to be noticed, to stand out from the crowd. You want people to learn your name. You want a personal touch."

Other trade show reps, he says, sat hunched at their display table, maybe staring at a laptop screen. "The good trade show booths saw people as humans. The bad ones were like ghost towns run by people who didn't care if you were alive or dead." When reps approached him with conversation, empathy, and kindness, he ended up more likely to cover the product in his writing, Brandon says.

The strategy is about more than just having an upbeat attitude, letting people know about product features, and welcoming people to a booth. It's a technique (hopefully genuine) that shows an understanding that people are busy and want personal attention. They don't want to be nameless. It takes one person at a time to have a successful trade show booth.

While a strong pitch is a start, it works even better if you couple it with a real-life look at the product. If possible, let visitors to your booth interact with what you sell. Offer demos, or iPads loaded with your software. Put three or four iPads on your stand and people will pick them up.

How Much Does It Cost?

Trade shows are pricey. A small booth can be $5,000 or more. That's just for raw space—you'll need to outfit that booth with rented tables, wall coverings, and other wares, quickly bringing the costs over the $10,000 mark and sometimes even exceeding $20,000. If you're traveling, those costs can add up quickly. Plus, you'll need to factor in any client dinners or other networking expenses you anticipate.

How Measurable Is It?

Very. As long as you research the event, trade shows offer certainty, because you are guaranteed to reach your target audience. Tracking sales that come from trade show interactions is generally pretty straightforward.

Qualified sales leads are not the only way to measure success at trade shows and events. Networking matters too. At one of the events WordStream attended, the team met marketers from a company with a similar target audience. Together, they scheduled and co-promoted a webinar. The result? More than a thousand sales leads, which the companies shared. "I've spent months trying to build the same relationships over email and the phone," Kate Gwozdz, a marketing specialist with WordStream, said. "But there is nothing like meeting someone in person and getting something on the calendar right there."

WordStream's Bumpy Road from Zero to Sixty Leads

FOR ALL ITS SUCCESS, WordStream, a software-as-a-service search engine marketing platform founded in 2007, had trouble maximizing trade shows. The Boston-based company hired marketing specialist Kate Gwozdz for the express purpose of gaining more qualified sales leads and boosting brand exposure at key industry events.

Success wasn't immediate—it grew out of some key speed bumps and lessons learned. Some of those lessons came from understanding the reality of the trade show floor. For WordStream, a key first step in qualifying sales leads is walking prospects through a free online tool. In any given month, between 60 and 70 percent of the company's qualified leads come from the free tool, which is called the AdWords Performance Grader. But at one key conference, the Internet connection was spotty at best. "For the most part we couldn't even get the bandwidth to make it run," Gwozdz recalls. Only twenty-nine attendees completed the free tool at the two-day event which, all told, yielded seven qualified sales leads. That's better than nothing, but less than ideal given the company's overall outlay on the event (including travel and accommodations) was $18,000.

One big problem: when the free tool was unavailable, suddenly there was no one in the booth who could quickly determine whether someone was a qualified lead by simply asking a few questions. The team didn't even consider that they'd need that skillset. "We just assumed we'd run them through the free tool," says Gwozdz. Because of that experience, the team learned to staff events with multiple sales reps who can react to any situation.

WordStream staff also learned the hard way to make sure their product was a fit for event attendees. This, too, probably seems obvious. But sometimes it's hard to assess the fit until you actually talk to potential customers. At one popular industry conference, it turned out that the attendees—sophisticated paid-search professionals—were a bit too advanced for WordStream's solution, which is designed for non-experts. Complicating matters, some attendees who wanted to try the software were stymied when they couldn't remember their AdWords login information—which meant they couldn't use the WordStream tool.

At that event, only twelve attendees completed the free tool in two days, and the company came away from the event with ten qualified sales leads. Still not the ideal ROI for an overall cost (including travel and lodgings) of $25,000.

By the time the next event came around, WordStream staff was ready. The staff created several simple forms that attendees could quickly fill out. One was a basic request for a product demo for those who forgot their sign-in info. Another allowed attendees to email a link to the free tool to the right colleague. Then there was a sign-up for the WordStream newsletter and a fishbowl for collecting business cards. It was a useful illustration of how bare-bones solutions can be best when all you really need in a trade show situation is an efficient capture of contact information. At the end of the four-day conference, the team had collected 160 cards. And, with multiple sales reps on hand, there were plenty of useful conversations between the WordStream team and the folks putting cards in the bowl. In fact, the sales reps took notes on the back of the cards. They wrote down their own name and the potential customer's biggest pain point. That way, the business card—in addition to providing basic contact info—contained knowledge that would help the sales team pursue the lead in earnest.

WordStream's total spend on the third conference—practically down the street from its headquarters—was $16,000. By staying local, the team not only saved money, it was able to staff the conference with multiple sales reps, facilitating lead qualifications and information captures.

In addition to the 160 business cards WordStream captured in the fish bowl, it generated 60 qualified leads at that conference—a sixfold increase from the previous event.

Guerilla Marketing at Trade Shows

No matter how valuable they can be, trade shows are simply too expensive for many young companies. But in many industries, they are hubs of potential customer activity. So why not crash one? With a little careful planning, it may be possible.

If you can, before the show, visit the main venues and surrounding hotels. Figure out where people will walk, pick up buses, catch cabs, have lunch, and meet for drinks. You're trying to find the best locations for maximum visibility. Along the way, suggests Don Rainey, general partner at venture capital firm Grotech Ventures, meet the bell captain in the hotels that are nearby but aren't part of the official show, say hello to the head of housekeeping and talk with the bar staff at local watering holes. These folks are integral players in the guerilla marketing game and can often make or break your campaign.

Ask your new friends crucial questions: Would the housekeeping, bar, or bell staff don a free t-shirt, hat, or button with your logo? Do any of the hotels have in-room programming and can you be included? A fundraising mantra comes into play here: If you don't ask, the answer is always no. No matter what, always stay clear of the things that are the purview of the trade show itself. You don't want to get yourself blacklisted from future shows. You just want to take advantage of the larger ecosystem around a show to get some visibility for your company. There is a lot of room for everyone around a big event.

It's not always going to work. And it's not for the faint of heart. But in some cases, the hotel staff will naturally assume someone else authorized you to replace the hotel's normal coasters in the bar with your logoed ones—maybe with the help of a tip for the bartender,

Rainey notes. You could try putting t-shirts on the bell staff, or find the popular bars in town and tape posters in the bathroom stalls. You can also send a team wearing your logo and take lots of pictures to post on social media to position your brand as part of the festival experience. Pass something out that's relevant to the event, or better still, fill a need that attendees have (soap, shampoo, relief from the noise). Be professional: Always bring a high-quality product or pitch, and enough inventory.

You want to execute your ploys in close proximity to one another and throughout the run of the show. As part of the action phase, expect some backlash. Trade show organizers may not take kindly to your antics. If someone gets mad, apologize and move on.

Whatever you do, don't expect to just show up at the trade show or event and set up shop. Most festivals and shows are strict about when, where, and how you can sell, so know the rules before you go.

GRASSROOTS MARKETING

When you think of grassroots marketing, you probably think, "cheap." It's true: Grassroots campaigns generally rely on word of mouth and organic, non-paid placement. But just because it can be done inexpensively doesn't mean it's for everyone.

For grassroots efforts to pay off, you generally need a super-targeted audience, says digital media strategist Samuel Edwards. If you're trying to engage Mexican Americans between the ages of eighteen and twenty-four who live in Tennessee and watch professional basketball, it's difficult to justify paid advertising that will target a much larger swath of the population. Grassroots efforts give you more control over your reach.

Grassroots tends to work when your audience craves interaction and personal attention. Think about a craft vodka maker canvassing local bars. That target market wants to think of themselves as discovering something new rather than choosing a beverage based on national ad campaigns. There's an inherent "coolness" to grassroots marketing that is particularly effective for certain kinds of products and markets.

Finding Customers

If your audience fits into those buckets, there are a few ways to get started. People are naturally curious. When they see a large crowd gathered on the street with signs and giveaways, they (almost) always stop. Sending out brand representatives to interact with passersby creates a more lasting effect than simply sending out targeted Facebook ads. That's particularly true in an era when people are glued to smartphone screens all day long. If you can convince them to look away from their mobile devices and interact with a booth or a pop-up event, the interactions tend to be memorable and effective.

Additionally, employing street teams creates a more personal connection to your brand. Most interactions now take place behind a screen; they're anonymous and impersonal. When customers have the chance to interact with actual people, they feel like they're heard and their opinions matter.

If your business has an enthusiastic niche customer base or audience, you can follow in the footsteps of marquee companies like Lululemon and Red Bull and use local influencers to market for you. Red Bull's "Wings Team," for example, is comprised of college students who market the brand's lifestyle of energy and excitement.

If you have enthusiastic fans, deploy them to the streets to pass out product, or send them to wherever your audience hangs out. They'll do more to establish credibility among their peers than you ever could.

Instead of simply being seen as middlemen between a company and its consumers, brand ambassadors give a company life beyond its corporate offices. You have to cultivate the relationships and set parameters, since these people are a reflection of your brand. It is imperative for you to spend the right amount of time recruiting, training, and building relationships with your ambassadors to guarantee their authenticity and resonance with your audience.

How Much Does It Cost?

A large part of the point of grassroots marketing is that it's cheap. The cost of some printed material, or some samples, and your time—that's all it takes.

Can I DIY?

Grassroots is made for DIY. It's all about your authentic voice, and connecting with customers and potential customers. While a marketing consultant can help you shape the idea, you want to be the face, and the boots on the street for the implementation.

Sam Adams Goes Grassroots for Decades

IN 1984, JIM KOCH founded the Boston Beer Company, maker of Samuel Adams Boston Lager. In 2007, he described to *Inc.* how his small brand outmaneuvered the big guys when it came to marketing. The lessons about connecting with people are timeless:

> Forget about media buying and ad agencies. If you're competing with people who have way more resources than you, traditional marketing isn't helpful. You have to start with a product— whether it's beer or software—that's meaningfully better or cheaper than the established competition. You also have to realize that it's going to take time to change people's perceptions. It took Sam Adams ten years to get national distribution.
>
> The next step is finding the consumers whose needs the product meets and educating them. It doesn't have to be a lot of people. We targeted imported beer drinkers in thirty bars in Boston. I learned that you need to convince not only the decisionmaker (for us, the bar's general manager) but also the influencers (the bartenders), and that you need a ten-second pitch that they can tell customers. Ours was: "Try this new beer: It's handcrafted in small batches. You'll like the taste."

When you're trying to educate consumers, do the small things that the big guys think are below them. For us, that meant table tents, promotional nights, and interacting with our target customers. Twice a week, I would go to a bar and talk to people about the beer. That helped me understand what kept people from drinking Sam Adams. I found out that people had an irrational attachment to imported beer that had little to do with the actual quality. So we put booklets on the bottles that explained why our domestic beer was better. The booklets cost 1.4 cents each—or about 2 percent of sales—but it was worth it. By our third year, we had distributed five million of them.

We didn't start doing TV ads until 1996, and they did not drive any noticeable growth. In the end, you can't fool customers into buying a product that's not any better than the next one. That's the province of well-financed companies. A small company has to be better and find ways—the more dramatic the better—to show consumers that it's better. Otherwise, go home.

Happy Family Takes Grassroots National

WHEN SHAZI VISRAM LAUNCHED organic baby food company Happy Family in 2006 (then called Happy Baby), all of her funding came from her own pockets or from family and friends. Without money for advertising, "we were forced to get creative," she told *Inc.*

The company printed a brochure explaining why organic food was important for babies and why Happy Family's organic foods were a healthier and better alternative to jars. Then the team of four scooped up the brochures and headed outside to parks and playgrounds, to talk to every parent and caregiver they could find. "We visited moms' groups and reached out to healthcare professionals. We hand-delivered products for sampling to local family and parenting media," Visram remembers.

While chatting up strangers wasn't easy, Visram says, she was heartened by all of the friendly responses and good wishes along the way. Local toy and children's clothing stores even agreed to display brochures. The brand grew and was eventually picked up by Whole Foods—a coup that put tremendous sales pressure on the small company. Knowing that "the mom-to-mom network was our greatest marketing asset," Visram says, they tried to figure out how to scale that model nationally.

It was the aughts, and the mommy blogs were proliferating. So, the company started sending out samples and information to bloggers, quickly gaining a following. Years later, says Visram, "we send samples of every new Happy product to mommy bloggers for product reviews and giveaways. We never turn down a request from a blogger no matter how small her following, and we are delighted to see an increase in dads who blog."

Today, Happy Family employs more than a hundred people, and its products can be found in major retailers across the country.

—

REFERRAL MARKETING

How did you find your dentist? Your doctor? A babysitter for your kids? The chances are high that you do business with someone who came recommended from a friend or family member. Customer referrals are one of the most powerful selling and marketing tools available: Eighty-three percent of respondents said they trust the recommendations of friends and family, the highest of any form of advertising, according to one study from Nielsen.[5]

Referral marketing, sometimes called word-of-mouth marketing, uses someone else's recommendation of a brand to bring in new business. Because loyal customers refer the brand to people they think will also like it, companies can reach the right customers with a message that's coming from a reliable source. Plus, referrals don't just lead to more customers; they often lead to better customers. Current customers know who would benefit from your company's services better than you ever could. They're also likely to talk up your company as they make referrals, making those newly referred customers educated and predisposed to loyalty.

When to Ask for Referrals

Before you put any sort of plan into motion, sit down and think about what you hope to get out of your referral program. Besides the obvious reason—getting more customers—what are you trying to achieve? Perhaps you're looking to increase customer loyalty, grow sales, turn more customers into lifetime customers or get more brand advocates. Once you identify the specific objectives, you can set key performance indicators to measure the success of your program.

There is a right time and a wrong time to ask your customers to help you market your product or service. If your business is one where a customer can quickly see the benefit of what they bought from you, then you should ask for a referral soon after the purchase, when they are still excited about the product. On the other hand, if you sell a product or service and the benefit of that is not clear for some time—say enterprise software—then the customer is not necessarily in a position to give you a referral immediately. It may take a long time for the customer to realize the benefit and be excited about recommending it. Keep in mind your product or service's life cycle before putting your plan together.

How to Ask for Referrals

Once you know the right time to ask for a referral, figure out how you're going to ask. Even when you already know a customer likes your company, asking for a referral can still feel awkward. You don't want to be seen as pushing for another sale (even though that's exactly what you're doing and need to do). You can soften the sales-y tone by focusing less on how customers can help your company and more on how you can help customers and their friends. Put the burden of facilitating the referral on you instead of the customer: Ask for their friend's contact information in a web form, send them a link to be shared via social media, or even offer a copy-and-paste message they can easily send to a friend.

One natural way to get started is to issue a survey as part of the post-sale process. Consider surveying your customers about a week after purchase, when feelings about your company—positive or negative—are still vivid. While any survey will help you understand your customers' sentiments, a question like this is valuable for referrals: "How likely is it that you would recommend [your company] to a friend or colleague?" If they say they would, follow up with a request for a referral.

Once you get customer feedback or testimonials, don't forget to incorporate that into your marketing materials and onto your website.

Adding an Incentive

Even if your customers really, *really* like you, it can be hard to motivate them to make a bunch of referrals. After all, people are busy, and their time is valuable. That's why many companies use an incentive. Often the most effective incentives have a cash value, such as a discount on your products or services, but they don't have to be monetary to work.

For example, Dropbox has an extremely successful referral program, and it doesn't carry a high price tag. In exchange for referring a friend, customers are given free storage space. Whatever you decide to do, make sure the incentive makes sense for your brand and for your customer. Put yourself in their shoes and think about what you could offer that would benefit them the most.

Once you select your incentive, publicize it. Create a central location where customers can get all the information about your referral program, such as a dedicated landing page on your website. When setting up the page, make sure it's easy to find. Make it easily accessible from your homepage by including it within your main navigation.

This page will be where you include your main message and call to action as well as all details about how to submit a referral. If possible, include a form right on the landing page to make submitting the referral even easier.

No matter what you give away, your referral program will only work if you have a great product to begin with. Your customers should be excited to channel their love for your product into a desire to share their great experience.

How Much Does It Cost?

The cost of a referral program comes in the setup, any web development or software, promotion you put against it, and of course, the value of the incentive that you're giving away.

Referral programs don't have to be expensive. A small discount on your product or a month free for a subscription service are powerful incentives—especially when your customers feel they're helping others get in on something good.

How Measurable Is It?

If you've set up the program carefully, you'll be able to garner great metrics. If you're mostly using your website to collect referral forms, set up analytics beforehand, so you're tracking completed forms and conversions. You'll need to know how people are getting to your landing page, including where they're coming from and what they clicked on. Once you know which channels are most successful—for instance, are most of your referrals coming from Facebook?—you can boost your efforts there. And if any channels are performing poorly, you can direct your efforts elsewhere.

Once you've built it, make sure they come. Come up with a schedule to promote your referral program across social media, email, and your blog. Use as many channels as makes sense to ensure you reach as many people as possible.

<<<<<< **CASE STUDY** >>>>>>

Tesla Gives Out Swag

DOES TESLA MAKE A great product, which generates tons of great press on its own? Undoubtedly. But that doesn't stop them from using current customers as marketers. Tesla's referral system works because they have a fantastic product, as well as infrastructure that makes it easy (and cheap) to refer new clients and reward existing ones.[6]

The exact rewards for current owners have varied over the years, but here's a recent example:

1 to 2 Qualifying Referrals:

A Signature Black Wall Connector or miniature drivable electric Model S for kids

3 Qualifying Referrals:

21-inch Arachnid Wheels for Model S or 22-inch Forged Turbine Wheels for Model X or

A week-long test drive of a new Model S or Model X

4 Qualifying Referrals:

Founders Series Powerwall 2—a red, limited-production Powerwall 2 home battery

5 Qualifying Referrals:

Invitation to the next unveiling event or early access to the company's coming Solar Roof

Clearly the most fanatical brand ambassadors are getting the greatest rewards. Offering a tiered rewards system keeps the company on their advocates' minds, and encourages them to talk with their friends about how much they love and would recommend their experience with the company.

The costs of the rewards items themselves are easily overshadowed by all the revenue that referred customers bring. Case in point: in late 2015, one Tesla owner referred 188 new customers, and generated around $16 million for the company in two months. That customer won a P90D Ludicrous Edition Model S.[7]

CAUSE MARKETING

Causes are hip. In 2015, 66 percent of consumers said they were willing to pay more for sustainable brands, up from 55 percent in 2014 and 50 percent in 2013, according to Nielsen.[8] The trend shows no signs of abating.

That's good news for your marketing. You can support a great cause and engender goodwill among your customers at the same time. It can be differentiating if you're in a crowded industry, and there's no underestimating the power of the feel-good factor. Imagine a software company supporting initiatives that get new technology into public schools, or a food delivery service donating its goods to homeless shelters. The possibilities are endless.

You may want to take a campaign approach, drumming up interest and publicity over a limited period of time. Or, you can consider making a cause (or causes) a core part of your marketing and product strategy. A charitable partnership that's aligned with your company's values has the power to strengthen your mission, foster a philanthropic spirit among staff, and may even turn your once-in-a-while customers into longer-term loyalists.

Try a One-Time Campaign

Start by determining how much you can afford to give away. Annual planning is a good time to think about supporting a cause, so you can incorporate into your budget how much you'll be giving away. You certainly want this to benefit your business, not hurt it.

To get everyone at the company involved and excited, you might want to ask your employees what cause they care enough about to want to get behind. Or pick something that has had an effect on your life or that's somehow related to what you do—a way to use your product in a charitable way, or to support a related cause. Or, you can align to a broader initiative that people are talking about, like Breast Cancer Awareness month, the Ice Bucket Challenge, or International Women's Day.

One of the simplest ways to structure a campaign is to give a percentage of all revenue generated from a specific product purchased for a specific time period. For example: *"All profits from our new software product for the next two weeks will be donated to the Columbus City Schools.* Or, you can donate dollars for each purchase made over some specific amount. An example: *"For any total purchase made over $200, we will donate $20 to the American Red Cross."*

If you're looking to collect information from customers, that's a perfect time to begin a campaign. You can donate dollars to a cause of your choice for each survey taken, up to a certain number of surveys. Janine Popick, founder of email marketing company Vertical Response, says when her company offered a $10 donation to the Susan G. Komen Foundation in honor of Breast Cancer Awareness Month for each completed product survey (up to 300 surveys), they hit their goal number in just two days.

Before you start the campaign, make sure you spend some time talking to the charity or funds recipient, too. Many charities offer free publicity as a means of enticing the support and sponsorships of businesses. If your company chooses to sponsor an event or organization, you may see your business logo plastered across t-shirts, social media platforms, and flyers supporting the cause. If the charity hosts an event, you can send a few employees and post pictures on your website and across social media.

Include the campaign in all of your marketing materials along with a link to the cause. Talk about your involvement on all your social networks, and use relevant hashtags. Once you reach a donation amount that feels significant, shout it with pride. Put it on your website and in your social networks. Talk about the amount of money you raised and what it was used for. You can also send a note to customers who participated, letting them know that their participation had a meaningful result.

Make It Last

If you want to incorporate long-term cause marketing, you can think about creating a partnership with a charity or nonprofit organization. No matter what organization you're considering, first ask yourself whether your company's vision, mission, and goals align with those of the charitable organization.

Marketing agency Inspira, for example, has a partnership with Alex's Lemonade Stand Foundation, an organization dedicated to fighting childhood cancer. Inspira not only works with the organization on many of its flagship fundraising events, but it also donates a portion of its profits to the nonprofit to aid in the fight against pediatric cancer.[9] The company chose that charity because it's a cause that hits close to home for founder Jeff Snyder. His daughter, Kennedy, was diagnosed with a rare form of spinal cancer when she was just two years old and has been battling the disease ever since. Inspira's charitable partnership drives its purpose, the employees it chooses to hire, and the campaigns it develops.

For many companies, there's an opportunity to donate more than just money—you could offer your product, or your employees' time. Coders could teach elementary school kids, or extra product could be sent to homeless shelters.

Consider BoxLunch, which belongs to a crowded market of novelty retailers. Through its partnership with Feeding America, the pop culture–themed retailer is working to chip away at the hunger crisis in the United States. For every $10 customers spend on its merchandise, BoxLunch provides a meal to someone in need. To date, it has supplied more than 14 million meals through Feeding America's food banks.[10]

The cause that customers can support through a product should align with your company's overall values. For example, Warby Parker works with a nonprofit that trains people in developing countries to perform eye exams and provide glasses at affordable prices to their communities. Since Warby Parker is a company that sells glasses, this initiative makes total sense. For example, if you sell a product like hiking boots, or sports clothing, it would make sense to support an environmental cause.

One cautionary note: Tread carefully when it comes to political or socially charged causes. Not only do you risk alienating potential customers, but employees as well. Any effort that involves employees should unite them and connect them at a deeper level. You can't do that if you're sowing controversy.

 ## How Much Does It Cost?

You control the cost of your campaign or initiative. Make sure the costs don't run away from you by electing to donate up to a certain dollar amount, or capping your contributions another way. You'll also need to consider the cost of any corresponding marketing.

For a long-term commitment, you'll need to build the cost into your business model. Adjust the frequency of these contributions as it fits your financial capacity, and make sure to stick to your word: If you promise to donate a meal for every $10 spent, as BoxLunch does, make sure you can commit to it.

Can I DIY?

Absolutely, and you should. Authenticity—a real connection to a cause—is a key element of cause marketing.

How Measurable Is It?

With cause marketing, it's not always easy to track and measure effects. Those who advocate for cause marketing say that beyond the warm fuzzy feeling it generates, it helps set you apart in a sea of competitors.

When you're running a cause marketing campaign, there are some things you can do to quantify impact: You can build some metrics into the initiative. Note how many social media followers you add. Track increased traffic to your site or store.

SWEEPSTAKES, GIVEAWAYS, AND CONTESTS

It sounds like a foolproof plan: Host a giveaway (everyone likes free stuff!) and you'll receive more sign-ups, likes, comments, and follows than you've ever had. Sales will spike because awareness for your product and brand will be so broad—and you will be profitable forever after.

Time for a reality check, says Jim Belosic, CEO and co-founder of contest company ShortStack. While giveaways can be incredibly effective for reaching business goals, they can also be a huge waste of time and money if you haven't prepared well. Belosic suggests asking yourself a handful of questions before you start the planning process.

Does the Prize Have Emotional Appeal?

While expensive prizes are what some marketers might call "sexy"—an all-expenses-paid trip to an exotic location or the latest Apple must-have—they don't guarantee success. The giveaways that do really well—those that get shared a lot and/or receive thousands of entries—are the ones that take their intended audience into consideration. The prizes speak directly to the needs, interests, and desires of the audience they're trying to target. Even better, they're relevant to the company and keep its products top-of-mind. One great example is a contest hosted by Tootsie Roll Industries, the iconic candy company. The prize? The opportunity to be a test-taster for a new Tootsie Pops flavor. More than 43,000 people entered that particular contest in just three days, says ShortStack's Belosic, whose company administered the contest.[11]

During your planning process, spend some time thinking about the kinds of prizes that will resonate with your audience. You could save money on what might have gone to an unnecessarily extravagant prize and you'll also help improve your giveaway's odds of attracting more of the kind of people you want to engage with—true fans of your brand.

Am I Asking Too Much of People?

People don't have a lot of time, and they don't want to give away lots of personal information. Keep in mind that people don't trust businesses to do the "right thing" with their personal information. *("Sure, asking for my email address is fine, but why do you need my phone number and zip code and marital status, too?!")* Ask for the bare minimum, like a name and email address. You save people time and engender goodwill by not requiring lots of personal info.

By simply reducing the number of fields in your form from six to three, you can increase your giveaway's conversion rate an average of 66 percent, according to QuickSprout.[12]

Am I Prepared to Execute?

When you're in the planning stages, it's easy to think that by the time your contest launches, executing it will be your top priority. Think again. What often happens for businesses running giveaways in-house is that the responsibilities of day-to-day business get in the way. This often shoves promoting the giveaway to the bottom of the daily to-do list.

To avoid this, automate your promotional efforts as much as you can before it even starts. You may be able to set up autoresponder emails to send to entrants at calculated times. You can also schedule social media posts to publish throughout the duration of your giveaway. The more you invest in marketing automation processes, the better chance your giveaway has of being successful.

What's the Post-Giveaway Action Plan?

You're going to collect a ton of data over the course of your giveaway. Use it. Think of every person who entered your giveaway as a brand-new lead. If you got your prize right, you attracted a highly engaged audience and they're not just leads, they're highly qualified leads. To make them work for you, follow up. Whether it's sending out a personalized and incentivized email, or commenting on each piece of user-generated content that was created to enter to win your giveaway, follow-up is a crucial step. Without these post-giveaway efforts, you're missing out on the real value of hosting a giveaway.

Making It Social

Social media is a natural place to hold a contest. But just because you post it doesn't mean followers will engage. Execute them carefully, though, and contests and giveaways have the tendency to spread like wildfire.

Timothy Sykes, the founder of an online stock trading academy, has built a massive social media following by offering periodic giveaways to his followers. He does this by asking his followers to answer a relevant trivia question about his content or business.

Timothy requires each follower who responds to tag two to three friends in the answer—doubling or tripling his reach. Sykes sends winners one of his products, such as a DVD program from his academy—and sometimes he gives away cash.[13] It's a great low-cost way to drive a lot more engagement.

Sweepstakes vs. Contests vs. Lotteries

It's essential to understand the differences between sweepstakes and contests (which are legal promotional campaigns), and private lotteries (which are illegal). A sweepstakes is a campaign in which entrants can win a *prize* based on *chance*. No purchase, payment, or other consideration is permitted, and the winner is picked at random. The element of *consideration* must not exist in a sweepstakes. What does that mean? Consideration is anything of value the contestant must give up to participate, monetary or non-monetary, and can exist if the contestant must expend substantial time or effort that benefits the sponsor. For example, some states have determined that providing contact information is consideration if the information is to be used for marketing purposes.

Contest for Good
at Cotopaxi

OUTDOOR GEAR COMPANY COTOPAXI donates 10 percent of its profits to charitable causes in the developing world: Buy a Kilimanjaro backpack, and you will be providing three weeks of tutoring to a child at an orphanage in Tanzania. Buy a water bottle, and you're helping a nonprofit called Charity Water dig a well near a school, enabling young girls to attend school and bring home potable water instead of spending their days going to remote wells.

It's an admirable mission. But when it comes to rugged outerwear and gear, consumers often are looking for the known brand name—the North Face coat, the Patagonia backpack. To build a brand in the space, Cotopaxi founder Davis Smith needed to think creatively and attract a loyal audience.

On the day of its launch in April 2014, Cotopaxi planned to hold a competition called Questival in Utah, where teams would compete for prizes by completing challenges like hiking or volunteering at a local soup kitchen. To encourage signups, Smith and his team went around to college campuses with their llamas—yes, their llamas—in tow. (Cotopaxi's logo is a llama—"They're rugged and they're the chillest animals you can imagine," Smith says.) A thousand people signed up to compete.

He didn't stop there. Each team was required to post pictures of its members wearing Cotopaxi backpacks in order to complete each challenge. This resulted in 30,000 social media posts during the first twenty-four hours Cotopaxi was up and running.

Today, the adventure challenge contests are a major component of the young company's marketing strategy, with dozens of them held around the country each year.

—

Isabel Harvey Lures Customers to Stores

ONE REASON THE MASSACHUSETTS boutique Isabel Harvey has thrived, say founders and sisters Kimberly and Alexis Kissam, are its promotional contests where customers are rewarded with discounts.

The Daily Glitter contest relies on the pull of urgency. Every day in December, Isabel Harvey sends its customers an email. Each email contains a discount offer redeemable that day only—that is, until the store closes for the night, or until midnight if you're buying online. For example: One day in December 2015, the email offered 30 percent off an Ethiopian leather tote bag. The email provided a picture of the bag, along with the proviso that it was available in two other colors. In addition, the email provided a discount code for online shopping, and a reminder that there was free shipping for all of December.

A different day, the email touted a "Buy 3 Get 1 Free" offer on Nicolette bracelets, which were depicted in a photo. It also included the discount code and the same reminder about free shipping.

Same-day promotions like this make it easy for the Kissams and their employees to gauge which discounts have the most appeal. Any retailer can tell you what "normal" Tuesday afternoon store traffic looks like, compared to what it looks like when there's a tempting discount on Ethiopian leather totes.

Plus, because it's all conducted through email, the Kissams can compile data about their open rates and the demographics of customers who use the discount code.

While the Kissams haven't precisely measured their average cost of customer acquisition, they have gained a general understanding that the contests are a far more efficient means of gaining new customers than, say, radio advertising, which they tried several years earlier.

Importantly, the giveaways in Daily Glitter are decidedly not bottom-of-the-inventory items. If anything, they are coveted items with the power to excite customers, bring spenders to the store, and cement the brand's reputation as a hip boutique stocked with hot items.

—

A contest is a campaign in which effort, skill, or merit, is required to enter to win a prize. For example, you may require people to upload a photo or video in order to enter. The winner is determined by voting or other judging criteria. The element of chance must not exist in a contest.

A lottery requires purchase, payment, or other consideration (the contestant has to buy something, such as a ticket), chance, and a prize. Private lotteries are illegal under state law. Under federal law, it is illegal for U.S. citizens to even participate in a foreign lottery. With all of these regulations—just don't run a lottery.

The Law Cares About Your Contest

Lotteries aside, administering any kind of contest is more complicated than you may think. That's because they're governed by certain laws you'll have to abide by, and the rules can be confusing. If you're thinking of hosting a contest or giveaway—online or off— you'll want to make sure you're following the laws where you live, and the rules laid out by the platform you're hosting it on. But that's not all you need to be aware of.

In the United States, companies need to make sure their Internet sweepstakes and contests don't run afoul of regulations around online gambling. The rules get very specific—and explain all of the fine print you see when you encounter a sweepstakes or promotion. Language like "no purchase necessary" and "void where prohibited" are legal requirements, and there are many others, including rules around the descriptions of prizes, entry procedures, eligibility requirements, and judging criteria. Make sure you talk to a legal expert.

Many states in the U.S. individually regulate promotional campaigns, especially when prizes include alcohol, tobacco, or firearms.

It is important to know that promotional campaigns are governed by the laws and regulations of the state in which the *contestant* lives. As you write your contest rules, take note that individual states have individual legal requirements that may include registration requirements or different rules for high-value winnings. Check with an experienced attorney before conducting any promotional campaign.

How Much Does It Cost?

A contest can cost as little as the item you're giving away and your time, if you're communicating it through channels you already use, like social media. If you'd like professional help, you may pay as little as $30 a month for an automated service from a company like ShortStack, or thousands for help from a full-service agency executing a splashy branded promotion.

Can I DIY?

Because of the complexity around the laws and regulations, we don't recommend it. Depending on the type of contest, a low-cost online contest administrator may be an option. There are lots of options, for example, if you want to execute the whole contest via social media—something like a simple social media photo contest.

How Measurable Is It?

Very—when done right. Make sure you have the infrastructure in place to capitalize on the leads that come in through the contest. You should be collecting information from everyone who enters, and putting those people into your marketing funnel. While

contests and sweepstakes often produce big numbers at the time—
some contest promoters will boast returns of a thousand percent or
more—that rush often doesn't last. Add participants to your distribution lists, and engage them through other channels.

SPONSORSHIPS

For a little-known startup, sponsoring an organization or activity
can be a valuable way to boost your credibility and name recognition. It's about cachet by association. That doesn't mean paying millions of dollars to emblazon your name on an NFL stadium. There
are lots of low-cost, low-lift ways for startups to get your name out
there through sponsorship.

Prize Donations

Prize donations are a top sponsorship opportunity for small businesses. They only cost as much as you want them to, they get your
business name out to a lot of potential winners, and they give winners the chance to try your product or service for free. If you have a
service-oriented business, you can donate gift certificates and show
off your valuable skills to winners.

Try to align to an organization with lots of potential customers
who may not have heard of you. For example, if you're a meal delivery service, offer a free week as part of a fundraiser at a school or
daycare. If you have a product-based company, consider donating
your goods to a related nonprofit (e.g., wetsuits to an environmental organization).

Other sponsorship options:

- Fundraisers

- Provide local meeting space

- Company day of service events

- Matching gift program

- Corporate grant program

Nontraditional Sponsorships

When you think of corporate sponsorships, the back of someone's shorts probably aren't top-of-mind, but in the world of mixed martial arts, it's just about the only spot that's readily visible—and clothed. For sponsors, that makes it the money spot, and, according to Bobby Harris, founder and CEO of BlueGrace Logistics, it's worth every penny.

Sponsoring a NASCAR team or having the company logo on the Green Monster in Fenway Park may be the dream of every sports-loving business owner. But for most, the hefty price tag for a major sports sponsorship is out of reach. Niche sports, by contrast, can offer a worthwhile marketing experience at a fraction of the price. "Dollar for dollar, you just can't compare the value," says Harris.

Since it was founded in 2009, BlueGrace Logistics, based in Riverview, Florida, has sponsored more than twenty fighters. Why MMA? Harris got the idea to sponsor fighters after a chance meeting with Ultimate Fighting Championship light heavyweight Jon "Bones" Jones in a hotel lobby in Las Vegas. Not yet a big fan of the UFC, Harris didn't know what to expect from someone who gets kicked in the head for a living. So he was pleasantly surprised to find that Jones was a smart, charismatic guy, who, Harris says, "holds himself like a champ."

That got him thinking. "I wondered how much it costs to endorse someone in the UFC," he says. As it turns out, not all that much—at least compared with other sports. According to Jones's agent, Malki Kawa, CEO of First Round Management in Doral, Florida, it can cost as little as $10,000 to sponsor a fighter for one night, and an annual contract starts in the low six figures. That's not pocket change, but it's a fraction of what a Nascar deal would cost.

For BlueGrace, which manages freight hauling and shipping for companies, MMA was a perfect fit. The company's marketing department did some research and learned not only that UFC fans are predominantly male, like BlueGrace's clients, but also that shipping managers in particular are highly likely to be UFC fans. What's more, UFC fighters' bonuses depend on their social media activity, which makes them some of the most Facebook- and Twitter-savvy athletes around—and great ambassadors for your brand.

Beyond guaranteed logo placement during fights, there are other advantages: BlueGrace's fighters, for example, have appeared on Fox and in the pages of *Maxim* magazine, all while sporting the company's logo. "That secondary marketing was completely unexpected," Harris says.

A Cautionary Note

Nontraditional sponsorships aren't for every business. UFC fights can be shockingly violent and may not project an image that businesses want to be associated with. Larry Rothstein, president of the New York City–based sports marketing firm Source Communications, says business owners need to consider worst-case scenarios.

For instance, when Rothstein took over Amtrak's sports sponsorships, he pulled the company's Nascar deal. "I never wanted to see a crash happen with Amtrak's name on it," he says. "MMA sponsorships are for companies with the ability to tolerate the violence."

There are lots of nontraditional sports to consider when it comes to sponsorships—from bowling, to surfing. Sponsoring these kinds of lower-profile sports may cost as little as $20,000 per event—not cheap, but a far cry from most professional athletics.

How Much Does It Cost?

Donating your space as an organization's sponsor, buying Little League uniforms or providing food or a giveaway can be a very low-cost commitment. Once you get into the realm of larger-scale sponsorships, particularly those with national reach, you'll likely move into the tens of thousands.

How Measurable Is It?

Measuring a sponsorship's return on investment is a challenge. However, because your key goals are to increase brand awareness and generate positive publicity, you'll get a sense when the initiative becomes a marketing success—or if it doesn't. As with all marketing, you'll want to identify the key performance indicators upfront, whether that's a survey to assess brand lift or a sales boost after an event.

PUBLIC RELATIONS

> " A good PR story is infinitely more effective than a front page ad."

RICHARD BRANSON,
Virgin Rebel: Richard Branson in His Own Words

Public relations is all about getting earned media—that is, earning free placements, as opposed to paid media. While there's no question that traditional media doesn't have the monopoly on clout and influence that it used to, there's still no substitute for a mention in the press, particularly in big national media, which tend to elevate the perception of your brand. For many companies, local publications or industry pubs may also be extremely valuable.

Similar to influencer marketing, with PR, you don't get to control your message. How your message is conveyed is up to the reporter or editor managing the story. PR always includes the risk that a reporter will decide to take an entirely different tack on the message you provided—and that's a risk that makes some businesses nervous.

While there's no question PR is great for spreading the word about a company—especially a young company that's trying to raise its profile—that doesn't mean that every press mention will translate directly to sales. It's often not that simple or direct. Because the media is established, much of PR's power is its ability to cement your company's reputation as "legit," and to lend credence to your brand.

So How Do I Get a Profile in *The Wall Street Journal?*

Every PR professional has been asked this probably a thousand times. If your goal is media placement, you can start by learning a bit about how reporters think and work. Just that knowledge alone will put you light-years ahead of your competition.

First, understand that while to you, your business is the most innovative and the greatest, reporters hear that dozens of times each day. Really. That's not an exaggeration. Reporters at big media outlets can receive two hundred pitches a day or more. So just saying you're the best isn't going to cut it.

Also understand that what you think is a story is different than what constitutes a story to a member of the press. Very few companies warrant dedicated profiles devoted to them. Reporters look for trends to talk about, or shifts in a marketplace, or a link to timely news. If you can plant a seed about how your company is representative of something new or shifting, or why you're qualified to talk about something in the news, you're starting to think like a reporter.

Connecting with the Press

Start by finding the right reporters to connect with. If you already know a reporter, maybe someone who has interviewed you before, start there. He may be willing to pass your name on to colleagues if he isn't interested. If you don't know a reporter, they're pretty easy to track down. Most reporters have "beats," or areas that they typically report on. Simply look at the bylines for articles about your industry. You're likely to see the same name or names pop up over and over. Then you simply send them a personal email explaining why you contacted them. Once you have a feel for a reporter's beat, you can tailor your message to that person.

Another approach to consider is the use of the "Help a Reporter Out" website—it's a network that pairs reporters with sources for their stories. In this case, you don't get to choose the story. Instead, after you sign up, you'll receive emails listing all of the stories journalists who use the service are working on. If you feel like you have the ability to comment, you reach out to the reporter directly.

If you're interested in a specific publication, take some time to study it. Look for the reporters who routinely have bylines about your industry or sector. If they can't help you, they may be willing to point you in the right direction.

If you're trying to connect with a reporter, first, consider what makes a story worth writing about. Remember, reporters are not customers. A sales message like "we can save you 25 percent on purchasing costs" isn't going to pique the interest of the media. Instead, a media-ready story needs a "hook" that makes it newsworthy, usually by attaching itself to whatever news stories have recently been gaining a lot of media attention. There's some art involved in figuring out story angles—it's not a natural skill for most business owners, and even for some PR professionals. You may consider hiring an out-of-work newspaper reporter, who can help you craft timely pitches. Sadly, there are plenty to go around.

Once you've defined a newsworthy story, you can figure out how your message might fit into that story. Remember, just because you pitch a certain angle doesn't mean a reporter is under any obligation to take it.

 ## How Much Does It Cost?

Freelance PR help can be found for as little as around $50 an hour, whereas working with a large, full-service agency can exceed hundreds of dollars per billable hour. Project-based agencies offer a "one price for all" payment structure that may cost as much as $10,000 a month, depending on the scope. Some PR pros (though not many), offer "pay for performance" options, where you only pay if they make a media placement for you—anywhere from a few hundred to thousands of dollars, depending on the outlet and the placement.

While it can get pricey, PR professionals have established networks of reporters and editors they work with, and they craft pitches for a living. If you know that press coverage is your objective, it can be worth the investment.

No matter what type of practitioner you select, be upfront about how much money you can spend and don't hand over money without seeing regular results. Establish a reporting schedule, request regular updates from a singular point of contact (if you're working with an agency), and offer enough direction to allow the PR pro to get the job done without micromanaging every detail.

Can I DIY?

In many cases, it's worth a try. Unlike other forms of marketing, virtually the only cost is your time, and the rewards can be huge. Many business owners who go the DIY route find they're most successful when they cultivate relationships with the right beat reporters, offering to help with stories. Then it may take some time to find the right way to work something in about your product or growth. But when you do, the dividends can be enormous.

Corcoran Invents Data—and *The New York Times* Bites

YOU DON'T HAVE TO be a big name to get high profile press coverage. Just ask real estate mogul—and *Shark Tank* star—Barbara Corcoran. Early in her career, she invented a data-driven report she called *The Corcoran Report*. The report calculated the average real estate sales price in Manhattan—but at the time, it was based on just seven total sales, because that's all the company had done. She crafted some introductory copy about conditions in the marketplace—"It sounded fancy," she says—and mailed the report to reporters at *The New York Times*.

Two weeks later, she says, she opened the paper and a story on the front of the real estate section trumpeted "New York City Prices Hit All-Time Low." And in the first sentence of the story—the "lede," in journalism parlance—the reporter wrote, "according to Barbara Corcoran."

She was stunned, she says. "I started churning out reports for the entire rest of my career," Corcoran recalls. Media members soon started turning to her whenever they needed a quote or statistic on the real estate market in New York. "When you're constantly quoted as the expert in your field," Corcoran says, "everybody believes that you are."

7

CUSTOMER MARKETING

HANGING ONTO CUSTOMERS IS harder than it's ever been. Consumers are bombarded with choices— they're savvier and more demanding—and loyalty is fragmented. Study after study has shown that consumers—particularly younger ones—are more willing than ever to abandon a brand in favor of another if they're offered something shinier or cheaper.

It's a well-worn truism that acquiring a new customer is harder and more expensive than hanging on to the ones you've got. So how can you do that, in a fragmented marketplace where loyalty isn't top-of-mind? Even if you're not in the customer service business, there's one clear way to please your customers: Act like serving them is your first priority.

Start with the basics. Stand in your customer's shoes. Look beyond your own business and understand your customer's full range of choices for everything that you sell. Take the time to really dig in, imagining the full ecosystem of options for your customers. This exercise will also deepen your understanding of competitors and help you better anticipate their moves.

Once you have a sense of the current landscape, spend a day in the life of a customer's order. Watch as the order moves through the pipeline, whatever your business may be. Track the milestones along the way, noting if the customer is receiving all the communication they should, if everything about the interaction is clear and easy to follow, and where the experience breaks down. Get as close to mirroring a customer experience as you can in order to experience the true hiccups in the process.

CUSTOMER SURVEYS

To figure out what customers want and if they're happy, there's a lot to be said for simply asking them. In order to serve your customers better, you have to know them better, says Laurel Mintz, founder and CEO of marketing agency Elevate My Brand.

Generally, you'll find that customers love giving their opinion and value being heard. Giving customers a place to talk about what's working and what isn't makes them feel empowered. For you, gathering the right information through surveys and questionnaires can help you analyze your sales process, restructure your business model, create more effective product design, and shape more effective marketing campaigns.

Email is an easy way to start. You can try soliciting feedback through your website, or you can send out an online survey. When a customer responds to an email form, stay in touch. Reassure them that they'll get a speedy response, suggests Mintz. Showing customers that you care about their experiences will help build relationships that give them a reason to stay. The same goes for surveys that you send out. If you can, send a personalized thank you and be clear about how much you appreciate their participation and what the feedback will be used for. You can also solicit quick one-question polls in social media, if that's appropriate for your customer base.

Depending on your industry, feedback software may be an option. A program may be able to send a survey out after every appointment or after each order is placed. "We can immediately see who our promoters are and who had a less-than-perfect experience, which gives us an opportunity to reach out before we might lose that person as a customer," she notes.

Once you've aggregated your customers' responses, use them. The information will help you create marketing campaigns that resonate and are effective, make decisions about future product positioning, and make any necessary changes to the ordering and fulfillment process.

Gathering buyer data is a useful exercise, but to really get to know your customers, you have to go deeper. Facilitating deeper, open-ended conversations may help you move forward if you're in a pivotal time for your business—whether you're facing new competition, launching a new product line, or opening a new location.

You may not be able to count on customers to come to you with constant feedback. But creating a forum for communication gives clients an opportunity to openly discuss both problems and successes on an ongoing basis, so you don't have to wait for an annual survey to find out what kinds of issues or concerns your customers face. "Recently, we launched a private Facebook group for our customers," notes Syed Balkhi, co-founder of conversion rate optimization software company OptinMonster. "The conversations we are having help us get to know customers on a personal level. The Facebook group is helping form a community where bloggers can help each other out, and they can also ask us questions in a more relaxed and casual way."

Or, take it in person. Host a lunch at your office for your best clients, or create a networking session.

How Much Does It Cost?

How much should you devote to existing customers? One guideline is to invest 10 percent of your marketing budget to talking to everyone in your marketing universe, whether or not they fit your ideal customer profile, suggests Peter Economy, author of several leadership and management books. Use another 30 percent of your budget to persuade people who do fit your customer profile—your prospects—that they should become your customers. Devote the remaining 60 percent of your marketing budget to your current customers. This is where you will produce the greatest profit for the least cost per sale.

CRM SOFTWARE

There's no substitute for talking to your customers. That's how you'll get the deepest, most actionable insights. But when it comes to day-to-day customer interaction, customer relationship management (CRM) software can ease the burden.

An effective CRM application provides an organized, comprehensive view of a company's customers and prospects, and employees' interactions with them. CRM software is hardly new, but prices have dropped dramatically in recent years, and usability has greatly improved. The key is to get everyone on the same system, and get them to use it. Nothing gets in the way of achieving a total view of the customer like having different departments use different products, or having some employees capture a lot of data while others never touch the system.

One way some companies solve those problems is to modify their incentive programs to reward employees not only for selling or otherwise serving customers, but also for gathering information about them. CRM software will capture extremely detailed information about customer behavior and preferences that can inform targeted marketing, product development, and sales activities.

CRM software can help you:

→ **Realize which customers produce the most profit.** By analyzing buying behaviors and other customer data, your business can gain a better understanding of who are your best customers. You can differentiate between the customers who provide the highest profit margins and those who simply bring you the most revenue. You could use that information to provide a better type or tier of customer service for better customers.

→ **Analyze buying patterns.** More understanding of customer buying patterns can help you spot potential high-value customers so that you can make the most of your sales opportunities with those customers.

→ **Maximize per-customer profits.** Data gleaned from CRM can help you lower the cost of selling to certain customers and help you increase profits from those customer interactions.

The ultimate goal is to use data in more than the usual who-is-buying-what or which-sector is-underperforming way. Instead, use data as a way to understand the full scope of a customer's problem, which can create opportunities to sell customers a broader, more integrated set of products or services. Or to simply be more confident that you know what their issues are, and you're as relevant to them as ever.

How Much Does It Cost?

Today you can find a CRM solution for as little as a few dollars per month—though that's pretty barebones. For a more full-featured suite, you may pay $50 per month or more. Salesforce, probably the best-known player in town, offers plans for as little as $25 per user per month for a simple, off-the-shelf solution; $150 for a customizable version.[1]

8

WRITING A MARKETING PLAN

YOU PROBABLY SPENT WEEKS—if not months—on your business plan, to provide a holistic view of the entire organization and how it will operate and grow. It's a prerequisite just to get a foot in the door with lenders and investors. You may have made a nod toward marketing in that document—and you may have thought that was enough. But while that's a start, for most growing businesses it makes sense to invest in the development of a separate, more-detailed marketing plan. The plan will be your roadmap to acquiring new customers and deepening relationships with the ones you have. It will serve as a north star, making sure as conditions change and you're making in-the-moment decisions, those decisions are grounded in a sound strategy.

The specific objectives of any marketing plan will vary depending on the nature of the business behind it and that business's goals. But most marketing plans consider a few fundamentals, like market and customer research, branding/positioning, competitive analysis, tactics, budget, and measurement. It's a lot to cover, but once complete, the document will serve as a comprehensive roadmap for your company.

For small businesses, it's best to think of a marketing plan as a way to tell a concise story that covers all the key points of your strategy going forward. So, keep it brief: The best plans can be told in 15 pages or fewer. Before you begin, it could be helpful to establish three items:

1. **A completion date.** A deadline you set in advance for *when* you want to complete your first draft of the plan. It's important to remember that establishing an effective plan will be an iterative process. You can count on your plan changing.

2. **The responsible parties.** Establish your team's roles and responsibility. In other words, make sure you identify *who* is doing *what* and *when* they need it completed.

3. **Your budget.** When it comes to putting together a marketing strategy, it's critical to establish ahead of time *how much* do you have to spend, as that can have a major impact on the strategies you decide to implement.

Once you have these items in hand, you're ready to put your plan together.

START WITH YOUR OBJECTIVES

The first step in developing your marketing plan is to establish the marketing objectives that will accomplish your business goals, says Karen Albritton, former CEO and president of Capstrat, a North Carolina marketing agency. "If your business goal is to grow revenue, what marketing objective will accomplish this? Adding more customers? More repeat customers? Higher expenditures?"

One of the steps you can take to create your objectives is to first create a vision statement, which is basically the long-term mission for your business that is both timeless and immediately inspiring for organization stakeholders. Every business has its own brand, so in setting your vision, you should identify the attributes of your product or service that define the brand and its long-term positioning.

Another step that can help set objectives is to perform a SWOT analysis, where you identify the strengths, weaknesses, opportunities, and threats facing your business. By conducting such an analysis, you should identify the key insights and strategic plans that will drive your business over the next one-to-five years. This includes understanding your five Cs—the consumer, channel, company, competition, and climate—deeply enough that when you finish, you should understand your point of difference in the market and where your opportunities lie, says Deb Roberts, marketing strategy consultant at Synapse Marketing Solutions. This should inform how you set your objectives.

Once you have your vision and a better sense of the opportunities and threats facing your business, you can begin establishing objectives. You want those objectives to be specific, measurable, attainable, relevant, time bound (SMART, get it?). That will help you drive to your tangible goal, such as profitable growth or market share.

A good plan requires simplicity, and simplicity requires focus. The key is to be realistic and specific, but also set a limited number of marketing goals related to what you think is your target market.

CONDUCT SOME RESEARCH

Many businesses fail to conduct the market research and market analysis that could really help them. "It's either overlooked or perhaps small businesses feel it is a cost they can't afford," Albritton says. Marketing plans that don't incorporate that kind of research, however, will almost certainly waste money. This goes back to what we talked about at the beginning of this book: better understanding who and where you customers are.

One of your primary goals in conducting research is to set focus areas, says Albritton. "It's easy to fragment your efforts without discipline," she says. "So set a clear definition for the type of customers you want." At this point you should tackle your priority geography or audience segment and begin focusing on the product and service offering you do best.

Strategies are the *how* in your plan, Albritton says. This is the point where you begin to address questions such as:

- → How will you position your business against other business?

- → What target markets are your best prospects to achieve your goals?

- → How will you price your offerings to achieve your goals?

Strategies should also be broad enough to capture several specific tactics, says Roberts, such as "build brand awareness" or "deliver unmatched customer service."

"Ultimately, all work done on the business should fall into these strategies," Roberts says. "If the work doesn't satisfy the strategies, then it shouldn't be done."

OUTLINE YOUR TACTICS

Tactics are the *what* in your plan, says Albritton. Start by thinking about what you should do first to achieve the best results. That may be as simple as putting together a very good presentation. Start small and build tactics one by one. For each tactic you develop, note how it fits your areas of focus, your strategies, and your objectives.

An example of a tactic could be, according to Roberts, to reduce days from order to delivery as a way to accomplish a strategy of "delivering unmatched customer service." If your strategy is to build brand awareness, tactics might include out-of-home advertising or an influencer campaign. The tactics are the vehicles that will be used to communicate the brand messaging to the target audience. This is the meat of your plan—what you'll use to build an implementation calendar.

You should also develop a forecast for each tactic: Identify the volume of sales that you expect to earn from each marketing effort, the cost of goods sold attached to that sales volume, the budget, and any other financial figure that you expect to achieve as a result of putting your plan into motion.

MEASURE EACH TACTIC

In solid plans, tactics are thorough, all the way down to details concerning execution and measurements of success, such as launch dates and expected reach, says Roberts. The point is that you need to begin measuring whether the tactics are successful at delivering your objectives. You may even choose to stagger your tactics so that you can evaluate their effectiveness and learn which ones work best for your business.

Units of measurement can range from web traffic to retail foot traffic to increases in sales volume, Albritton says. Basically, you should strive to measure anything you can track to judge whether a tactic has made a difference.

Strategies vs. Tactics

The meat of your plan will include your objectives, your strategy, and your tactics. Putting tactics ahead of strategy is an extremely common mistake—not just at startups, but at all kinds of businesses. You may have a gut feeling that Facebook marketing—the tactic—is where you want to put most of your energy, but you can't be sure until you justify that decision with a strategy. The strategy has to come first—it's the "why" that leads to each tactic.

Here's an example:

Strategy

Become a leading industry expert in the area of software for schools, ultimately using that credibility to cement relationships with district leadership and drive sales.

Tactics

- Influencer marketing campaign distributing software to top education bloggers

- Content marketing including establishing a weekly blog on issues in education and contributing guest posts to high-profile education blogs
- Booth at top education trade shows

DEVELOP THE PLAN AND STICK TO IT

Your plan is only as good as its implementation, so also create a plan for precisely how you are going to execute on it, Albritton advises. Where appropriate, look to partner with other organizations to help with implementation. You may be able to find interns from nearby universities, for example. "These days, even high school students have amazing talents in technology and design," she says.

If your plan includes advertising or events, sometimes the vendors will help with implementation. Depending on your area of business, you may also consider bartering services with other businesses. If you don't currently have the resources available to take action, find someone who does.

IMPLEMENT THE PLAN—BUT STAY FLEXIBLE

Never forget that the opportunities and risks you established in your SWOT analysis might dictate that the objectives you've established in your plan might not happen "as planned," Roberts says. A whole host of variables could come into play that you never considered in the beginning, such as changes in consumer demand, channel expansion, customer contracts, competitive responses, and supply costs.

That's why the best advice is to rough out a plan and then put it down in detail with action items on a monthly calendar, Albritton says. Set a time to review the calendar each month, assess results, and determine next steps.

> " Measure or it didn't happen. CMOs face new marketing channels all the time, while overall budgets are mostly flat. This creates a need to laser focus on the ROI of all marketing activities. Today's top-performing channel is tomorrow's thud."

JEAN-LUC VANHULST, *President, Write2Market*

9

SETTING
A BUDGET

THERE'S NO SINGLE BUDGET figure that works for every business. How much you should spend depends on where you are in your growth and on what industry your business operates in. One commonly cited rule of thumb is that the amount you spend on marketing per year should range anywhere from 1 percent to 10 percent of sales—or possibly more, depending on several factors, including:

→ **How established is your business?** If no one has heard of your business yet, you may need to spend more to gain traction early on. Some experts recommend spending as much as 15 percent of sales early on.

→ **What industry are you in?** Every industry is different, and some are more reliant on marketing than others. You should have a sense of how much your competitors are spending.

→ **How much can you really afford?** Don't spend yourself into a hole that you can't dig out of.

How I'd Spend It—What Five CEOs Would Do with a $10,000 Marketing Budget

"I would hire a social-media marketing consultant to develop a strategy and fine-tune our brand on the residential side of our business. I'd train a couple of people on how to manage that ourselves, so we're not relying on a consultant to do that work. I'd also hire, on a part-time basis, a graphic designer, just to spice up our photos and the content we post."

–Michael Parnell, MP Consulting

"Direct mail–it's a hidden gem. Everybody thinks it's old school; nobody focuses on it anymore, which provides more opportunity for those of us who do. People who open up mail are a specific demographic. If your product fits in with the responsible, middle-aged group who typically open their mail, direct mail can be huge."

–Jim Carlson, Zurixx

"First, look at internal data about your customers. Using that, develop specific customer identities. One we've used is 'head of a regional media agency seeking a competitive advantage but who lacks resources for a video team to serve his customers.' Second, ask if you are communicating to your customers what you do in a non-confusing way. Third, spend money on the basis of what you found out in the first two steps. Figure out where your customers are when they have their buying hats on: events or social networks? Then create content that fits each particular environment. For YouTube, video; for events, a special kind of talk that is geared toward informing the customers you're looking for."

—Bettina Hein, Pixability

"I'd go to all of our partners, whether they're sponsors or the mayor's office, and I'd look at co-op marketing. To the city, I'd say, 'Let's run a joint ad for the festival and the city and try to double or triple that marketing budget and create some social media.' It's all about stretching the dollars."

—Danny Hayes, Danny Wimmer Presents

"If I was a new lifestyle company, I'd spend it on branding. Having a strong creative with a really crisp point of view that is timeless and stands out, and that you feel reflects who you are as a company, provides huge bang for the buck. You're going to live with your logo for a long time."

—Amanda Hesser, Food52

MAKE IT IRON-CLAD

When you're in the weeds executing your marketing plan, it's easy to experience creep—making on-the-fly decisions that result in increased spending on a campaign or initiative. That's why your marketing budget needs to be set in stone. That will help you make decisions with discipline, making sure every dollar counts and you're making appropriate tradeoffs.

To help you stick to your marketing budget, try these steps:

Create a Main Budget Made Up of Smaller Budgets

Your overall headline number is how much you want to spend on all marketing initiatives. But beyond that, it's important to have a smaller picture of how you want to dole out the funds. If, as you measure, you find that a particular tactic is underperforming, you can reallocate your buckets.

Plus, having specific buckets will allow you to get granular when it comes to tactics like social media campaigns, where you're paying for clicks or impressions and it's easy to get carried away.

Get Specific

Try not to rely on ballpark figures, but really home in on a specific amount you want to spend on each of your tactics or initiatives. That will give you a hard line when you're negotiating with advertising providers or agencies. Plus, when you have an exact dollar figure for each campaign, you tend to follow it more closely than if you're less specific.

Since marketing often comes with hidden costs, such as research, message testing, or further click purchases, being specific will force you to calculate the possibility of unforeseen costs into each plan and prioritize which ones are essential.

Track Your Spending

Just because you said you would only spend x amount of dollars on a campaign does not mean you actually did—those unexpected costs can stack up quickly, and all of a sudden you're thousands of dollars over what you planned for. If you're tracking as you go, you can make sure there is no overspending.

Be Ruthless

As you monitor your tactics, you will notice patterns that tell you which ones are working and which are underperforming. If you can, take the opportunity to tweak your campaigns. But don't hang on for months. If something isn't working, you want to avoid throwing good money after bad—something that can be tough if you've been planning a certain tactic for months or even years. If you can quickly identify the underperforming platforms, you can remove them and save that money, maintaining your budget target.

Many high-growth small businesses spend more than just a few percentage points on marketing because they know the outsized impact it can have when you're establishing a brand or gaining traction for a new product. But not everyone has the cash flow to do that. A small business with a small marketing budget needs to get attention and drive sales on a shoestring. This means getting creative.

BUT I HAVE NO MONEY

Businesses that are very good at marketing themselves with very little money tend to do a few things very well. First, they focus on building a large network of fans and followers to promote their business via social media. They put a lot of time and energy into engaging their fans and keeping them engaged, day in and day out. But they don't stop with social media—they harness energy for real-life connections, too. Depending on the business, that may mean knocking on doors, chasing referrals, or attending industry events. They build and maintain relationships with decisionmakers.

Successful low-cost marketers also never forget the value of current customers. They look after their existing customers extremely well, every day, all the time. That means constantly engaging with them to make sure they're happy and the products are working for them. When they can, they tap those customers for referrals.

They also may partner with other businesses that share similar customers and cross-promote. Think guest blogs, shared webinars or events, promoting each other on email and social media, etc. When you align with others, you get double the audience. If you're a retail store and it's Small Business Saturday, for example, find another small store in the area with a complementary product and consider doing a cross-promotion of each other for the day. Thinking this way reduces the cost of marketing for new businesses and accelerates the speed at which new customers come on board due to the existing credibility with the referring partner business.

Most of all, these founders and company presidents market all the time, regardless of how busy they may be. It's just a part of who they are.

WHEN TO MIX IT UP

WHEN IT COMES TO marketing, the world moves fast. On average, marketing leaders today say 34 percent of their budget is spent on channels they didn't know existed five years ago—and they expect that to reach 40 percent by 2019, according to the 2017 Salesforce State of Marketing report.

So how do you know when it's time to rethink your marketing strategy? The most obvious way to tell is when a strategy that worked without fail two years ago suddenly is falling flat—or your results have been gradually trending downward. It's particularly common these days in a universe of rapidly evolving social media. If you find that a tactic that worked like gangbusters is suddenly failing to convert, or you hear customers talking about a new social media site they're using all the time, it may be time to reconsider your marketing strategy.

That's not the only time you'll want to revisit your strategy. If you've introduced a new product or added new features, that's a great time to evaluate whether your marketing needs a bit of evolution. Plus, even if everything's going well with your marketing, you'll probably want to take time out once a year or so to dive deeply into your strategy and see if any tweaks make sense. Maybe you've had shifts in revenue, or you've found traction with one segment and not with another—taking time to dive deeply into your marketing and sales data may give you insights that lead to fresh takes on your marketing strategy.

BACK TO THE BEGINNING

You can start by going back to your personas. Has your audience changed at all? Have you discovered that your actual customers are a bit different than what you expected—a different age, concentrated in a different location, or at a different point in their lives? What's driving your customers to make the purchasing decision? Just as important—are there personas who aren't buying from you, but should be? Once you align your personas to actual behavior, you may notice trends or subtleties that you didn't anticipate—that many of your customers are moms who are on social media when their kids are in school, or that your marketing is performing particularly well in urban locations.

Once you have updated personas, go through the same exercise you did at the outset. Make some educated guesses about how each one is likely to react to different things you might try. For instance, if one of your personas lives in the suburbs and commutes to work, you might think that radio advertising during morning and evening drive times is an effective way to reach that person. If another persona is very focused on family, then tying your marketing efforts to holidays might be a smart approach.

When you're revisiting your strategy, you have the advantage of data that you didn't have when you were first starting up. You likely have detailed sales records and know which times you did better and worse. You also should have detailed records of promotions you tried and what advertising you ran when. You should know when you adjusted prices up or down and what impact that had on sales.

Next, test your hypothesis in the real world. Does your data suggest that a slight price drop will lead to a sharp sales upturn? Then try dropping prices in a limited-time offer without changing anything else, and see if that idea holds true. If it does, you've learned a valuable lesson about how price-sensitive your market is. Same goes for marketing shifts. If you see a spike in social media activity in the pre-bedtime hours, try targeted ads that reference bedtime, or post links to your content then.

The more you create and test hypotheses this way, the closer you'll be to your customers' actual behavior, giving you an actionable understanding to make changes.

LISTEN TO YOUR SALES TEAM

You have a critical source of data within your walls—your sales team. Feedback from those feet on the street can help you determine if your messages are reaching your target. Formally or informally, your salespeople are collecting data every single day. *Do certain blog topics or titles glean more qualified leads than others? Do certain video topics bring in very few qualified leads while others are immensely popular with prospects?* Lead number and quality data can help to optimize content and attract not only more leads but a higher percentage from the ideal audience—those who are more likely to convert into paying customers.

It's a great idea to bring your sales and marketing teams together weekly to review results from your current marketing initiatives. You want to ensure that your marketing is optimized to reach your target audience—the audience your sales team is connecting with every single day. A simple collaboration—even as informal as a weekly lunch—will align marketing and sales efforts, creating open communication and generating creative ideas for new marketing tactics or deployment to attract qualified leads.

When you're talking to your sales team, think in terms of audience need—the bedrock of contemporary marketing. Ask your sales team what kinds of questions prospects ask and what their true needs are. If your product is financial software and your key audience is struggling with keeping certain financial records in the cloud, maybe you want to publish an article or video series about archiving financial records. When sales teams are conditioned to have an ear to the ground for customer problems—and marketing teams are set up to hear that feedback and act on it—your customers and prospects get great value and you get closer to the results you want.

No matter what your industry is and what marketing tactics you're using, take a test and learn approach. Go back to the KPIs you set when you outlined your marketing strategy. Different channels and tactics will take different amounts of time to gain traction, of course, but after a few months you should see trend lines you can act on. If you use mostly content marketing, for example, your traffic should be steadily increasing, people should be linking to your content, and you should be converting on your site from your content. If you use Instagram, you should have steadily growing numbers of followers, and after a few months, those followers should be converting into fans who are visiting your website or coming into your store.

One of the hardest lessons for any marketing team—but especially one that's scrappy and young—is knowing when to cut bait. Not everything you try is going to work. Just because Instagram marketing is on the cover of magazines or everyone's talking about content marketing at conferences doesn't mean it's the best tactic for your company, your products, or your target audience. If you've worked iteratively and tweaked the execution a few times over a few months, and you're still not seeing meaningful results, it's time to dig into the data and rethink the strategy.

Creating Sales Collateral Your Sales Team Actually Uses

In almost every industry, the discipline of sales has changed dramatically in the last decade. While deals are still done on golf courses and over three-course lunches, today's consumers are hyper-informed coming into the sales process in just about every industry, changing the role of the sales professional. They no longer lean on salespeople for all of the product information. Instead, they want context and problem solving.

Marketing teams think they've taken steps toward solving for this shift. They're commissioning white papers and publishing audience-first content. But salespeople don't always use what marketing is creating. In many organizations there's a disconnect. Prospects aren't picking up the phone after reading a white paper, or the sales team doesn't find the materials marketing creates to be very helpful, and they don't even use them as part of their sales process.

It's a problem across industries and company sizes. In a 2017 Forrester study, 44 percent of B2B companies said that marketing and sales departments had a weak relationship when it comes to sharing knowledge about customers' buying process.[1] What a waste. Marketing and sales should be the most symbiotic of business relationships—particularly now, when customers are clamoring for solutions and marketing is better equipped than ever to provide them, rather than just pushing out messaging.

Fixing this problem starts simply: by talking. We already beat the drum of marketing and sales sitting down together periodically, and we'll reemphasize that here. Just getting together periodically and running through what's working and what's not, and what kind of product and marketing plans are in the pipeline, will start getting the two teams on the right, shared path.

But don't stop there. For marketing to generate high-quality leads for sales—and isn't that the whole point?—the two teams need to agree on the target markets, decisionmakers, and influencers, and have a shared appreciation of the buyer needs, buying process, and budget. They need to work together on the competitive advantages.

Then, the teams should analyze what they've been producing and working with. How do customers and prospects respond to different types of content or messaging? What does the sales team really think about the content, tools, and resources provided? What is working for them? How can these tools be made more useful? What's missing? What will help the most with closing deals?

Once the teams do that, marketing will have a better understanding of how sales is approaching the market—and sales will be better positioned to articulate the type of marketing collateral that will land in prospects' hands, instead of in the garbage.

———————

FINDING OUTSIDE HELP

THE *MAD MEN* **ERA** ended a long time ago. Shopping for an advertising agency is no longer done in smoke-filled boardrooms and martini bars—and the industry is vastly more diverse and splintered. Today, thousands of wildly different agencies exist, from five-person startups in Brooklyn to enormous traditional firms with a global reach, and everything in between.

The idea of expertise has changed, too. While having a great tagline or a slick TV ad may still be important considerations to some, for smaller companies a more focused expertise on social media, or content marketing, or experiential marketing may make more sense.

No doubt, in the beginning you'll probably bootstrap your own marketing, reading books like this, scheduling lunches with friends who are marketing types, and to some degree, winging it on gut feeling. Most startups have been there. But for most emergent companies, a partnership with an advertising agency is an unavoidable step in the growth process.

"The likely path for entrepreneurs is to experiment to some degree with advertising," says Tom Finneran of the American Association of Advertising Agencies (4A). "But entrepreneurs have such a full plate that they recognize that while they can do certain experiments themselves, when they start encountering significant investments, they need to have affiliations with experts. Just as that might be true for working with technology partners or manufacturing advisors, it's also true for advertising services."

Of course, simply deciding you need an advertising agency doesn't mean the search will unfold effortlessly before you. While agencies maintain the ultimate responsibility of winning your business, a large part of the search process—from understanding the best advertising options for your audience to choosing appropriate agencies for your business—falls squarely on your shoulders.

IS AN AD AGENCY RIGHT FOR YOU?

If you need to shift strategies fast, or if you need to connect with an audience and aren't sure where to begin, or if your marketing has sputtered, or if you're in the midst of a period of aggressive growth, bringing on an agency might be the right decision.

Writing a check isn't going to magically solve all of your problems. Before beginning the search, a small company needs to think critically about what role an agency would play in your business objectives. Whatever the reason—whether you're planning for accelerated growth, redesigning your brand, or branching into new territories—it should be fully formed before you first reach out to agencies. It's not the agency's job to hash out your business objectives; it's their job to craft a marketing strategy that aligns to those objectives and helps you reach them. So know what you're trying to do before you begin the search.

Working with a marketing agency, especially for the first time, should not be an impulse decision. Plan for a search that could take weeks and even stretch into months, much like an executive hire does. Whoever you select will hopefully be around for several years. Even if they're not located within your walls, they are an extension of your team. You want to take your time making the decision.

As you search, you may find that the agency landscape feels fragmented. These days, many agencies have a very specific expertise that may not meet all of your needs. Most large companies work with multiple agencies—a big company may have one agency for digital marketing, one for branding, one for social media, and one for advertising—plus an in-house marketing team. While that's probably not going to be the case for you, you can still find ways to benefit from working with multiple niche agencies that offer really specialized expertise.

If you find you really click with a highly specialized agency that can't meet all of your needs, that doesn't need to be a deal-breaker. You may be able to work with a couple of niche agencies who excel in a certain area—a content marketing agency and a traditional ad agency, for example, or a digital marketing shop and a branding agency. Any agency worth its salt is accustomed to working as partners with other, complementary agencies on behalf of its clients.

Before making a decision on any agency hire, consider the time you are willing to dedicate to this partnership, the money you're willing to invest, the skills your team already possesses, and the skills your team lacks. Your agency relationships should take you out of your comfort zone a bit—they should bring strategies and ideas that your team couldn't have produced on their own. They should challenge your thinking and continually refine and sharpen it.

WRITE A REQUEST FOR PROPOSAL

Once you've addressed the tough questions about why an agency is right for you, it's time to see how a few agencies think. A request for proposal (RFP) is the most common way companies share a little bit about themselves and your advertising objectives, as well as any financial requirements or contractual stipulations that make your request unique.

When expressing your vision, try to be realistic. "The small marketer that says I need an ad in the Super Bowl with no concept of the costs or how that money may be used more prudently in other manners is not based in reality," says 4A's Finneran. "That's a problem." The realistic scope and direction of your marketing stems from a clear understanding of your business model, your customers, and your prospects. No one knows more about your business and your customers than you do, and it's critical that you pass that knowledge on to any potential advertising partner through your RFP.

That means being very clear about your target audience, so the agencies who are vying for your business come back with a clear, targeted proposal that you can judge. If you're wishy-washy about your target audience, an agency isn't going to be able to clearly tell you whether they'd prioritize social channels, content marketing, or out-of-home. But if you say your target is men in their twenties who live in urban areas and commute on public transportation, you'll get a much more focused proposal for you to evaluate.

WHITTLE DOWN YOUR LIST

With an RFP in hand, it's time to start the actual search. Remember that agencies come in all shapes, sizes, and colors: There are thousands of them, and they are constantly changing. Instead of plunging in blindly, enlist the help of your peers. You can talk to other business owners to see what agencies they've considered or are familiar with. If you belong to an entrepreneurs' group, that's a great place to start because they're likely to recommend agencies who are adept at working with startup, high growth firms. You can also research via trade associations and dig into the marketing and advertising industry press to look for promising upstarts or specialized agencies.

There are dozens of criteria with which to narrow the agency field, but perhaps the most fundamental choice revolves around whether a small or large agency fits the needs of your company best. It's not always the case, but a smaller agency may feel more comfortable for a smaller company. Smaller agencies tend to have more accessible executives and be easier to navigate. That may come, though, at the expense of the very buttoned-up, hyper-professional approach and documentation you'll get from a bigger shop. Plus, established big shops have often worked with large brands and bring a host of experience they can apply to your work.

MEET THEM IN PERSON

Meeting with agencies can be intimidating, but you'll feel more comfortable if you do a little homework. These meetings allow you to really see how an agency works from both a creative and a business sense, so it's important to make sure you ask any questions or express any concerns to get all the answers and assurance you need to make a final decision.

Before the creative discussion begins, certain legal technicalities such as confidentiality, idea ownership, fees, and non-compete clauses need to be addressed and negotiated. An agency can't give you a thorough, well-thought-out pitch if they don't have all of the relevant information, which includes details about your product and market. That makes some founders squeamish, for sure, so make sure you have a rock-solid confidentiality agreement in place; consult your lawyer at the start.

Once you've gotten the legalities out of the way, it's time for more creative conversations. Often, first meetings between advertisers and clients are called capabilities meetings because advertising agencies demonstrate what they feel they do best—you may hear someone from an agency refer to their "capes." This is your chance to see where an agency believes they shine. They'll probably try to tell you that their capabilities are broad in scope—this is a sales pitch, after all—so dig into what they're presenting and make sure you're comfortable.

To assess the skills of certain agencies, ask for case studies demonstrating the agency's past projects. Keep in mind that case studies are not meant to exhibit their experience in your industry, but the creative team's overall style. Is it safe, or does it push boundaries? What's the tone? You can ask for examples that may be relevant for an audience or a strategy that you're considering.

While assessing the abilities of the agency you're meeting with, also take the time to assess the people in the room. In any meetings with a prospective advertising agency, stress the importance of meeting with the actual team who will work on your campaign to determine if you have the chemistry to make this partnership work through good times and bad. There will be stressful, high-pressure moments. You want to feel comfortable with the team—hopefully they'll be with you for the long haul, as you grow.

Keeping It in House: Dollar Shave Club

Agencies aren't right for all young companies. Dollar Shave Club founder Michael Dubin described to *Inc.* why he decided to hire full-time marketing staff rather than sign on an agency:

> By late 2014, something started to shift in the company. You get to a point—usually it's between fifty and eighty employees—when you need to start bringing in some process and organizational discipline. As the CEO, you have to realize you can't do everything yourself anymore. And teams need strategists, but they also need the right layers above and below to execute in specific areas. And I don't mean stacking people on top of one another hierarchically. I'm talking about ever-deeper layers of specialization and focus.
>
> Around this time, I started up an internal creative agency. We needed to build a really robust campaign for our first made-for-TV spots, which poked fun at how hard it can be to get into the "razor fortress" in most retail locations. I found some entrepreneurial creatives who could do more with less—we still had to be pretty scrappy—and an incredible project manager who could keep us on track.
>
> A lot of companies outsource much of their creative work. We don't. We wanted this expertise in-house precisely so we could be nimbler. This small group has grown to about twenty people. I still lead the team, help brainstorm, and give final approval, but instead of doing 75 percent of the work, like I did in 2013 and 2014, now I'm involved in probably about 20 percent of the work.

Our viral videos are basically our bible, and they help the team maintain our unique voice. The marketing has probably been the hardest thing for me to delegate as we've gotten bigger. It's tough to realize that you need to hire people who can do things better than you, especially when you have some expertise in a particular area.

Then again, it's also challenging to hire people for positions that you have no expertise in. I made that mistake with my first senior engineering hire, back in 2012. I just didn't understand the necessary qualifications because of my own inexperience. It became clear pretty quickly that it wasn't a good fit. Ultimately, if you want to build a big company, you need talent for every department that matches the much higher level you see at more mature companies. The more experts you have, the faster you can move. Instead of doing the work yourself, you have to shift into a role of inspiring and motivating people to drive the right results. It's one of the most important shifts a startup needs to make on the road to becoming a big company.

———

UNDERSTANDING MARKETING SOFTWARE

SOFTWARE ISN'T A PANACEA, but for a cash-strapped young business, the right tools can accelerate and bolster your marketing strategy. The trouble is figuring out where to start in a marketplace flooded with options.

Most founders are aware of customer relationship management tools like Salesforce or Hubspot, which we discussed in Chapter 7. They offer broad suites of tools for your sales and marketing functions. But there are dozens more. The available options are vast—and some tools are quite low-cost, or even free. Here are a few that are highly regarded in key marketing functions.

WEBSITE AND ANALYTICS

When it comes to your website, you'll probably start with Google Analytics. Most businesses do, large and small. The free tools from Google Analytics allow you to see which of your pages are performing best, and how users are navigating your site. It's an incredibly valuable tool to see if your customers are interacting with your site the way you thought they would.

To go deeper, with Optify, your website will be benchmarked against others in your industry, with feedback helping you determine areas where you can improve. Advanced analytics will give you all the information you need about those who visit your website, including the sites referring those visitors and what actions they take once they arrive at your site. This information could be just what you need as you start a new marketing campaign.

Some CRM tools that you may already be using, like Hubspot, also offer web analytics as part of an integrated suite of products. Hubspot also offers a pretty robust free version showing where site visitors are coming from and which pages are converting that many startups may find sufficient as they're getting off the ground. Plus, on Hubspot's site you'll find some really killer marketing resources for free. Whether you're looking for some creative site design ideas, a course on content marketing, or even a guide to effective blogging, chances are you'll find it among HubSpot's free marketing tools.

SOCIAL MEDIA MANAGEMENT

Staying active on social media takes time, and time is one commodity many entrepreneurs lack. Hootsuite is one popular tool that helps to monitor posts across various social media accounts. You can schedule posts to go live on multiple platforms at once, giving you the convenience of writing all of your social media messages at a time that works best for your schedule. You can also schedule posts to go live at a time when your followers are most likely to see them, rather than when you happen to be online.

Buffer is another free platform: It has all the important features you expect with a social media management platform, like post scheduling, baseline analytics, and the ability to customize posts for each social network. It also offers a browser extension so you can quickly and easily share what you're reading online without logging in to each of them.

Boosting your social media audience can help amplify each message you create and send. Followerwonk is a tool from Moz that helps you identify followers who are most likely to be interested in the type of content you offer. You can also research your existing followers to learn more about their interests and goals to better identify the type of content you should be sharing. This has the added benefit of giving you insight you can use when searching for new followers.

SURVEY DEPLOYMENT AND MANAGEMENT

Chances are, at some point you'll want to send out some kind of customer survey or questionnaire. SurveyMonkey is arguably the most popular tool in the space. The platform offers a robust free option where you can design and send slick, professional-looking surveys to your email list. The software also includes an analytics tool to analyze their answers.

What makes SurveyMonkey really useful is their expert-reviewed templates and questions to make sure the data that you're getting will be accurate and helpful—not skewed because of the way you worded your question or answers.

>>>> **CONCLUSION**

VIRGIN GROUP FOUNDER Richard Branson built an empire by staging stunts and generating worldwide attention. Barbara Corcoran spent years establishing herself as a real estate expert in New York City and cultivating a symbiotic relationship with the press. Dollar Shave Club invented an entirely new way of selling a standard drugstore commodity by making funny videos and making sure the right people saw them at the right times.

It's easy to gloat about the single viral video that took off or the guerrilla tactic that yielded a major customer breakthrough. But as the reporters and editors at *Inc.* have interviewed thousands of successful entrepreneurs over the years, we've learned that's not how most small companies hit it big. Instead, you can trace their success to, among other things, a rigorous, well-thought-through marketing strategy that was executed over the course of months—or more likely, years.

Richard Branson never delegated control of his social media accounts, despite running a global empire, because it would undermine his distinct voice and the rugged, in-your-face authenticity of his brand. Barbara Corcoran developed proprietary research reports, worded them carefully, and distributed them religiously, like clockwork, year after year. Dollar Shave Club founder Michael Dubin deliberately delayed announcing the company's new funding deal so the announcement would correspond with its video launch—dramatically increasing the likelihood that anyone reporting on the funding would discover the video.

In other words: Commercials look slick and tweets feel casual. But behind those executions are marketing strategies that take groundwork and effort.

For many new company founders, that may come as a surprise. They believe passionately in their product or service and want it to speak for itself. But the reality is that even the most breakthrough, effective, earth-shattering product can't gain traction without garnering some attention—preferably, lots of attention—from the right people.

No single expert can—or should—dictate your marketing strategy. But if you follow the steps in this book, you'll be well on your way to discovering what your brand stands for and how you can communicate that to customers and potential customers. The hardest part is getting started. In the words of that brilliant marketer Richard Branson, "Screw it, just do it."

>>>> **SOURCES**

Introduction

1. https://www.slideshare.net/gueste94e4c/dropbox-startup-lessons-learned-3836587
2. https://www.quora.com/How-did-Warby-Parker-gain-its-initial-traction
3. https://www.slideshare.net/HubSpot/jumpstart-inbound marketingv2

Chapter 4

1. http://www.nielsen.com/us/en/insights/reports/2017/2016-nielsen-social-media-report.html; http://www.pewresearch.org/fact-tank/2017/11/02/more-americans-are-turning-to-multiple-social-media-sites-for-news/

Chapter 5

1. https://www.forrester.com/report/You+Dont+Need+A+Social+Marketing+Strategy/-/E-RES133541
2. https://www.wordstream.com/blog/ws/2017/02/28/facebook-advertising-benchmarks
3. http://www.wsj.com/articles/lacroix-bubbles-up-in-sparkling-water-brand-competition-1460047940
4. https://adespresso.com/blog/instagram-ads-cost/
5. https://www.millwardbrowndigital.com/pinterest-and-the-power-of-future-intent/
6. https://blog.pinterest.com/en/150-million-people-finding-ideas-pinterest

7. https://www.reuters.com/article/us-snapchat-users/snaps-older-
   user-base-slowly-growing-ahead-of-ipo-analyst-idUSKBN15N2DG
   ?type=companyNews
8. http://www.prnewsonline.com/ibm-snapchat-keating
9. https://www.wsj.com/articles/youtube-tops-1-billion-hours-of-
   video-a-day-on-pace-to-eclipse-tv-1488220851
10. https://www.law.com/americanlawyer/almID/1202784834121/
11. https://www.hubspot.com/marketing-statistics?_ga=2.177618149.
    137038297.1510930128-441520748.1510157296)
12. http://www.adweek.com/digital/marketing-to-millennials-and-
    the-necessity-of-social-brand-advocacy/#/
13. http://blog.influence.co/instagram-influencer-rates/
14. http://phx.corporate-ir.net/phoenix.zhtml?c=176060&p=irol-
    newsArticle&ID=2185161
15. https://www.npr.org/sections/thesalt/2017/01/18/509675621/
    not-just-a-crock-the-viral-word-of-mouth-success-of-instant-pot

Chapter 6

1. http://adage.com/article/digital/digital-ad-revenue-surpasses-tv-
   desktop-iab/308808/
2. http://www.nielsen.com/us/en/insights/news/2014/music-360-
   americans-make-music-their-top-entertainment-choice.html
3. http://www.nielsen.com/us/en/insights/news/2014/for-advertisers-
   radio-is-worth-listening-to.html
4. *BtoB* magazine, State of Event Marketing, 2011
5. http://www.nielsen.com/us/en/press-room/2015/recommendations-
   from-friends-remain-most-credible-form-of-advertising.html
6. https://www.tesla.com/support/referral-program
7. https://www.autoblog.com/2016/01/03/
   teslas-referral-program-worked-like-gangbusters/
8. http://www.nielsen.com/us/en/press-room/2015/consumer-
   goods-brands-that-demonstrate-commitment-to-sustainability-
   outperform.html
9. http://inspiramarketing.com/blog/2015/spot-the-warrior-lemon-
   in-wilton-this-weekend-to-help-fight-childhood-cancer
10. http://www.boxlunch.com/boxlunch-gives/
11. https://www.shortstack.com/blog/how-an-iconic-candy-brand-
    used-a-giveaway-to-create-awareness-for-a-new-product/

12. https://www.quicksprout.com/2014/02/24/how-reducing-options-can-increase-your-conversions/

13. https://www.facebook.com/timsykesfans/

Chapter 7

1. https://www.salesforce.com/solutions/small-business-solutions/overview/

Chapter 10

1. https://www.slideshare.net/G3Com/b2b-buyers-mandate-a-new-charter-for-marketing-and-sales